A PATH MADE BY WALKING

Process Work in Practice

A PATH MADE BY WALKING

Process Work in Practice

Julie Diamond, Ph.D.
Lee Spark Jones, Ph.D.

Second Edition

BELLY
SONG
press

Santa Fe, New Mexico

Published by: Belly Song Press
518 Old Santa Fe Trail, Suite 1 #626, Santa Fe, NM 87505
www.bellysongpress.com

Managing editor: Lisa Blair
Cover design: David Moratto
Interior book design: Heiko Spoddeck

First published in the United States of America by
Lao Tse Press in 2004. This second edition
published by Belly Song Press in 2018.

All names of clients and facilitators
(other than the authors) have been changed.

Printed in the United States of America

Publisher's Cataloging-in-Publication Data

Diamond, Julie, author. | Jones, Lee Spark, author.
    A path made by walking : process work in practice / Julie Diamond and Lee
Spark Jones.
    Second edition. | Santa Fe, NM : Belly Song Press, [2018] | Revision of
the first edition (Portland, Oregon : Lao Tse Press, c2004). | Includes
bibliographical references and index.
    ISBN: 978-0-9998094-0-2 (paperback) | 978-0-9998094-1-9 (PDF) |
978-0-9998094-2-6 (Kindle/Mobipocket) | 978-0-9998094-3-3 (ePub) |
LCCN: 2018935358
    LCSH: Psychotherapy. | Counseling. | Mind and body therapies. | Jungian
psychology. | Psychotherapists--Training of. | Psychotherapy--Methodology-
-Cases. | Body-mind centering. | Dreams--Psychological aspects. | Change
(Psychology) | Mind and body. | Self-help techniques. | Human information
processing. | BISAC: PSYCHOLOGY / Psychotherapy / Counseling. |
PSYCHOLOGY / Movements / Jungian.

LCC: RC489.M53 D52 2018 | DDC: 616.89/143--dc23

1 3 5 7 9 10 8 6 4 2

Contents

Caminante, no hay camino,
se hace camino al andar.

Walker, there is no path,
the path is made by walking.
—Antonio Machado

Preface to the Second Edition

It's been 14 years since we published this book, and 17 years since we conducted the training workshop on Process Work in Sydney, Australia, which led to the creation of this book. To capture the development of Process Work in those 17 years would not just warrant the writing of another book but possibly two or three. For in those 17 years Arnold Mindell has continued to expand and develop the tools and concepts of Process Work, as he has throughout his remarkable career.

While we wish we had the capacity to include those developments, we will leave that task to others and instead devote our efforts to making this textbook available in other languages to reach more students and practitioners. As we look forward to that possibility, we are very grateful to the many teachers who used this textbook as part of their curriculum, across many disciplines, from counseling psychology to coaching to conflict resolution.

We hope the book you hold in your hands inspires you along your path of learning.

—Julie Diamond
—Lee Spark Jones

Acknowledgments

This book owes its existence to the founder of Process Work, Arny Mindell. His pioneering work and heartful intelligence has enriched our lives both personally and professionally. We dedicate this book to him with gratitude for his life-changing work, his delight in discovery, and the spirit of learning that he embodies. We hope that readers will feel that spirit in the pages of this book.

We also owe a great deal to colleagues and friends who have written, taught, and expanded Process Work over the years. Thanks to their dedication and creativity, over the past 20 years Process Work has grown from a radical new theory to a mature, multicultural paradigm of individual and social change. *A Path Made By Walking* stands on the shoulders of a few people in particular, whose research, published work, and teaching have contributed fundamentally to the thinking and practice described in this book. Great appreciation goes to Joe Goodbread, whose inventive intellect has been a prime mover in the development of Process Work. We are grateful to Amy Mindell for her synthesis of Process Work theory, her introduction of "metaskills," and integration of creativity and Process Work. We also are indebted to Max Schupbach, who has contributed so much to Process Work around the world through his teaching and wide-ranging application of its methods. We are thankful to Process Work students and seminar participants around the world, whose engagement in learning the methods and theory has helped us to understand Process Work in greater depth and detail.

Many people have helped us bring this book from thought to page. We would like to thank Joe Goodbread, Kate Jobe, and Sonja Straub for their valuable comments and suggestions. Stan Tomandl, Ioan Mitrea, and Elke Frensch made helpful contributions to early drafts of the book. We appreciate Willis Barnstone's willingness to discuss the translation of the lines of Antonio Machado's poem, from which the title of this book is drawn. We thank him for permission to use his translation. Sara Hollwey's inspired editing and enthusiastic support gave this book the final push it needed to make it into print. Many thanks also go to Leslie Heizer, Francie Townes, and Stan Tomandl for their help in the publication process. Heiko Spoddeck of Lao Tse Press was a tower of strength, whose attention to detail, hard work and commitment brought the book through its final stages of production. We are more than grateful to everyone who has helped us bring out the best in this book. Any errors that remain are ours.

Finally, we thank Molly, Nigel, and Ranger for their willingness to miss out on some of their daily walks, and then for getting us up and out, and reminding us to smell the salmonberries. Our deepest appreciation goes to the deep green beauty of the Central Oregon Coastal Ranges, which nourished us throughout the writing of this book.

—Julie Diamond
—Lee Spark Jones
Yachats, Oregon
August, 2004

Introduction

How does something new, exciting, even numinous, emerge from an old problem or difficult disturbance? When life brings painful experiences, or problems feel overwhelming, being able to find meaning in difficulty is liberating. Such transformational experiences often seem magical. This book puts the magic in your hands. Step-by-step, it details skills and attitudes that allow the magic to come through you, in working with yourself and others.

Process Work is a "path made by walking."[1] It begins with the stuff of everyday life: problems and preoccupations, delights, hopes and dreams. Large or small, obvious or barely perceptible, everyday experiences hold worlds within themselves, and mark the beginning of journeys into the unknown. Process Work methods provide a detailed, signal-based system of tracking, mapping, and unfolding the flow of momentary experience, or "process." Travelling the path of an unfolding process allows you to venture beyond the bounds of preconceived notions, familiar experience and everyday identity, and still find your way home.

An originally positive psychology, Process Work grew out of Arnold (Arny) Mindell's research into body phenomena and

---

[1] Antonio Machado, "Campos de Castilla, Proverbios y Cantares XXIX." In *Border of a Dream: Selected Poems of Antonio Machado*, translated by Willis Barnstone. (Port Townsend, WA: Copper Canyon Press, 2004), 281.

Jungian dreamwork in the 1970s. At a time when psychopathology was still the focus of much psychological practice, Mindell developed an awareness modality that went beyond the dichotomy of health and sickness. He coined the expression "the dream happening in the moment," to convey the idea that a numinous background to everyday reality manifests all the time, in a multitude of ways. In his development of Process Work, he provided conceptual and practical guidelines for bringing awareness of this "dreaming" reality into everyday experience.

Process Work is centered in a multidimensional awareness, which acknowledges the world of night-time dreams and the "dreaming" world long recognized by mystics and indigenous peoples, as well as the world that is generally consented upon as "real" in contemporary societies. Viewing experience with this kind of multi-leveled of awareness is like looking through a kaleidoscope. Each time you look through its viewfinder, you see changing shapes, colors, and patterns, which make up a uniquely coherent whole. Using this kind of awareness, you can see parts of yourself that everyday consciousness normally keeps hidden from view. Instead of erecting boundaries around a unitary "true self," it affirms your spontaneous, multi-faceted, and diverse nature, and encourages it to unfold in its own way.

Why we wrote this book

In Quantum Mind, Mindell uses the analogy of Alice's explorations in Wonderland[2] to describe Process Work as a journey into the unknown or "dreaming" aspects of existence.[3] Since we began practicing Process Work, like Alice, we have embarked on a journey that has turned our notions about our selves and the world around us upside down. No matter how many years we have been doing Process Work, we still feel delighted by

---

[2] Lewis Carrol, *Alice's Adventures in Wonderland* (Chicago: Rand McNally), 1950.

[3] Arnold Mindell, *Quantum Mind: The Edge Between Physics and Psychology* (Portland, OR: Lao Tse Press, 2000).

unexpected plot twists, surprised when something fun or creative emerges from a thorny problem, and enriched by diversifying our ways of looking at the world.

In July 2001, we were teaching the basics of Process Work at an intensive training seminar in Sydney, Australia. We began by mapping out, on a white board, the micro-steps of following a process, from the initial description of a problem, through to the emergence of something new and unexpected, and the integration of its meaning into everyday life. The group began to add to the map, until the activity became a collaborative effort and a multi-leveled diagram emerged. Seeing this mapped out in front of us, and buoyed by the group's enthusiasm for it, we were motivated to write this book.

We thought at the time that this would be relatively easy to do, by simply filling in the details of the diagram. Although the actual writing of the book grew into something more complicated, that naïve expectation got us started. We wrestled with concepts and techniques, trying to deepen our own understanding, and to describe simple steps precisely and in context. It is not always easy to describe a paradigm from within, especially one that is still creating itself. We found that knowing something as second nature was not a good precursor to explaining it. By returning to the basics of Process Work, we often found the keys to unlock what we wanted to say. And our love of learning and teaching Process Work kept us going until the book was finished.

About this book

This book presents our view of Process Work, its history, concepts, and techniques, based on our experiences as learners and teachers. It is not a definitive version of Process Work, because indeed there is none. In this book, we focus on the basics of working with individuals. Other applications of Process Work, including work with relationships, groups, and organizations, and advanced methods for working with individuals in altered states of consciousness, are not covered. For in-depth treatment of these areas, we refer the reader to the bibliography at the end of the book.

In the spirit of Machado's poem, Process Work is itself still in a process of emergence. We know that as soon as the last word of the final chapter is written, another book will be needed to fill in what this one leaves out. As of this writing, there are perhaps thousands of practitioners, teachers, students, and admirers of Process Work. True to the spirit of process, each one understands and practices the work in his or her unique way.

This book presents the history, concepts and practice of Process Work. Chapter One tells the story the conceptual development of Process Work, in the context of Mindell's life. Chapter Two explains key Process Work concepts, illustrated with examples of interactions between a facilitator and a client. Chapters Three through Eight focus on skills and attitudes central to the practice of Process Work. They include stories, examples, tips and exercises to convey how Process Work is used in working with individuals, and to help the reader learn through practical experience. Chapter Three describes the dynamics of process structure as a flexible framework for tracking the flow of experience, and for identifying "dream doors," or ways of accessing a dreaming process. Chapter Four introduces techniques for amplifying sensory-grounded information, and describes how to work with feedback. Chapter Five introduces unfolding techniques that focus on working with roles and "dreamfigures." Chapter Six introduces sentient approaches to unfolding, which use altered states of consciousness to access dreaming realities. Chapters Seven and Eight explore ways of integrating dreaming experiences into everyday life.

In life, a person's process rarely follows a tidy path of stage-by-stage development, and does not lend itself easily to linear explanation. So, in describing the various stages of following a process, this book presents an artificial picture, a kind of fiction. Although breaking a process down into smaller segments is not a true rendering of its nature, it makes learning and skill building more manageable. We hope that by the end of this book, the reader will have a clearer sense of the origins of Process Work, an understanding of its background assumptions and principles, and an appreciation of the basic, yet elegant, tools it has to offer.

Chapter 1

The Story of Process Work

Process Work is an evolving modality, itself a "path made by walking." Its development is best understood as Arnold Mindell's lifelong quest to piece together the mysteries of human consciousness, physics, and psychology. Starting out as an attempt to incorporate physical experiences and body symptoms into Jungian psychology's primarily dream-based method, Process Work has grown in unforeseen directions. It has become an awareness modality with applications in areas such as organizational and community development, diversity and leadership training, and spiritual practice, as well as individual psychotherapy, relationship counseling, and group work.[4] This

---

[4] For a recent account of the development of Process Work theory, see also Amy Mindell, "A Brief Review of Recent Evolution In Process Theory," *The Journal of Process Oriented Psychology*. Vol. 9, 1, Summer 2004, 60-66.

chapter tells the story of how Process Work has developed so far, in the context of Mindell's life and ideas.

A graduate student in physics at the Massachusetts Institute of Technology, Mindell arrived in Zurich, Switzerland in 1961, a few months after Carl Jung's death, to conduct research in theoretical physics at the Swiss Federal Polytechnical Institute. After complaining to his roommate that he was having bad dreams, he began therapy with Marie Louise von Franz, one of Jung's most devoted students, and a leading Jungian analyst at the time. Mindell's fascination with dreams led him to change careers from physics to psychology. Deciding to become an analyst, he entered the Jung Institute, and also began analysis with Jung's nephew, Franz Riklin. After graduating from the Institute, he worked in private practice, and later became a training analyst at the Jung Institute.

Mindell was always fascinated by dreams and dreaming. Yet his background in theoretical physics, and his deeply practical nature, brought a pragmatic flavor to his approach to unconscious phenomena. When he first began therapy with Von Franz, he was very skeptical about dreams. As a scientist, he had trouble believing that dreams could be meaningful. Von Franz challenged him to disprove this proposition by using his background in physics to understand psychology. Inspired by the challenge, Mindell wrote his thesis on Jung's theory of synchronicity, or the theory of non-local connections. He explored how one's inner experience could be connected non-locally to outer events through meaning.

Although he eventually became a skilful dream analyst, Mindell was not satisfied with interpreting or discussing the meaning of unconscious material. He was more interested in living it, in exploring and experimenting with the living unconscious. As he says in *Quantum Mind*:

> The idea that there is something called an unconscious around, within, or between us made me crazy for years. It sounded like the mysterious ether people used

to believe in before the discovery of relativity. I could not see the unconscious. Was it static or moving? What should I look for?[5]

Mindell wanted to put his hands on the unconscious; he wanted to find out what it looked like, how it felt, how it appeared in three-dimensional reality. He wanted to "give it feet,"[6] to develop a method of working with the unconscious in the here-and-now, in sensory-based and tangible ways. As he says, he "got frustrated talking about the unconscious. ... I wanted to live it and experiment with it more directly."[7]

Jungian psychology has a daughter

Mindell's own physical health problems gave him the opportunity he was looking for. While working as an analyst, he suffered from symptoms that drove him to study widely in the fields of health, disease, traditional and alternative medicine, and bodywork. He experimented with bodywork approaches and medical treatments. While he found some physical relief, he was not satisfied with the fragmentation he felt in treating his physical problems with methods that were not theoretically compatible with his psychological approach. As a Jungian analyst, Mindell was committed to Jung's teleological approach, the idea that dreams had a meaning or purpose. He thought that body symptoms, like dreams, must contain meaning and purpose for the individual. In his words, "I could never completely buy the idea of pathology. After studying Jungian psychology you have the idea, or rather the experience, that events are meaningful. The idea that I should think of myself as being sick

---

[5] Arnold Mindell, *Quantum Mind*, 438.

[6] Mindell has often used this expression as a way to convey the importance of finding hands-on methods for spiritual or psychological principles.

[7] Arnold Mindell with Amy Mindell, *Riding the Horse Backwards: Process Work in Theory and Practice* (New York: Penguin, 1992. Reprint. Lao Tse Press: Portland, OR: 2002), 8.

if I had a pain in my leg didn't feel right. ... Since I've always considered my dreams meaningful, I thought that maybe what was happening in my body was meaningful too, not pathological or wrong."[8]

Unexpectedly, as Mindell was grappling with this theoretical problem, and with his own symptoms, he visited a client who had been hospitalized with stomach cancer. Mindell tells the story of how his experiment with the idea that symptoms could be meaningful led him to discover the Dreambody concept:

> A patient with whom I was working then was dying of stomach cancer. He was lying in the hospital bed, groaning and moaning in pain. Have you ever seen somebody who is dying? It is quite sad and terrifying. They flip quickly between trance states, ordinary consciousness, and extreme pain. Once, when he was able to speak, he told me that the tumor in his stomach was unbearably painful. I had an idea that we should focus on his proprioception, that is, his experience of the pain, so I told him that since he'd already been operated on unsuccessfully, we might try something new. He agreed and so I suggested that he try to make the pain even worse.
>
> He said he knew exactly how to do that and told me that the pain felt exactly like something in his stomach trying to break out. If he helped it break out, he said, the pain worsened. He lay on his back and started to increase the pressure in his stomach. He pushed his stomach out and kept pushing and pressing and exaggerating the pain until he felt as if he were going to explode. Suddenly, at the height of his pain, he shouted out, "Oh Arny, I just want to explode, I've

---

[8] Ibid, 7.

never been really able to explode!" At that point he switched out of his body experience and began to talk to me. He told me he needed to explode and asked if I would help him to do so. "My problem," he said, "is that I've never expressed myself sufficiently, and even when I do, it's never enough.

This problem is an ordinary, psychological problem that appears in many cases, but with him it became somatized and was pressing him now, urgently expressing itself in the form of a tumor. That was then end of our physical work together. He lay back and felt much better. Though he had been given only a short time to live and had been on the verge of death, his condition improved and he was discharged from the hospital. I went to see him afterwards very often, and every time he "exploded" with me. He'd make noises, cry, shout and scream, with absolutely no encouragement on my part. His problem was clear to him; his ever-present body experiences made him acutely aware of what it was he had to do. He lived for two or three years longer and then finally died having learned to express himself better. What it was that relieved him I don't know, but I do know that the work relieved his painful symptoms and helped him to develop.

It was then, also, that I discovered the vital link between dreams and body symptoms. Shortly before he had entered the hospital, the patient dreamed that he had an incurable disease and that the medicine for it was like a bomb. When I asked him about the bomb, he made a very emotional sound and cried like a bomb dropping in the air, "It goes up in the air and spins around sshhhsss…pfftpff." At that moment I knew his cancer was the bomb in the dream. It was his lost expression trying to come out and finding no way out it came out in his body as cancer, and in his dream as the bomb. His everyday experience of the bomb was his cancer; his body was literally exploding with pent-up expression. In this way his pain became his own medicine, just like the dream stated, curing his one-sided lack of expression.[9]

Mindell named this mirroring of physical experiences in dreams "the Dreambody." He described the Dreambody as a dream-like, unifying field that gives expression to body symptoms and dreams alike. He published his first book on this concept in 1982, entitled *The Dreambody: The Body's Role in Revealing the Self*. A few years later, he presented his idea of the Dreambody in a lecture to the Jungian community in Zurich. Seeing his work as a development within Jungian psychology, he called his lecture, "Jungian Psychology Has a Daughter."

A quantum leap forward

When Mindell presented his Dreambody idea to the psycho-therapeutic community in Zurich, he showed its connection to Jungian psychology, and also to bodies of knowledge outside modern Western science, such as Taoism, alchemy, shamanism, and indigenous cosmologies. Although "Dreambodywork," as it was called then, was still firmly based in the Jungian concept of teleology, this daughter of Jungian psychology was well on her way to independence.

The development of Dreambodywork took a quantum leap forward when Mindell began to design a signal-based method of following process, or the flow of experience. Working with his colleagues, he studied videotapes and applied his scientific thinking to investigating precisely how a process unfolded, and how it could be worked with to reveal its

---

[9] Arnold Mindell, *Working with the Dreaming Body* (London, England: Pen-guin-Arkana, 1984. Reprint. Portland, OR: Lao Tse Press, 2002), 2-4.

implicit meaning. Mindell developed a detailed technology for tracking how experience manifests through multiple "channels," or modes of representation. This enabled him to apply the Dreambody method beyond the limits of individual "talk therapy," to such areas as movement work, inner work (self therapy), relationship work, and group work.

This was an exciting era of experimentation and development. Weeklong seminars on body symptoms, childhood dreams, chronic symptoms, inner work and meditation, were held in the Swiss Alps. Late into the evening, Mindell and his students gathered around a table in a local restaurant, brainstorming and dissecting the techniques and concepts of the work. During this period of growth, each class, seminar and workshop became an exhilarating quest to discover the structure behind the mystery of process. The pull of ideas, the excitement of trying new things, and the sense that some mystery would be revealed just around the corner, all lent a sense of urgency to that time.

After several years of focusing primarily on body symptoms and dreams, including chronic symptoms and their connection to childhood dreams, Mindell extended Dreambodywork to include any type of disturbance, including conflicts, moods, complexes, and relationship problems. He coined the phrase "the dream happening in the moment," to convey the idea that all experiential phenomena are manifestations of a dreaming reality, and can serve as ways of accessing non-ordinary consciousness. As Dreambodywork expanded its focus to include all kinds of human problems, the work became known as "Process-oriented Psychology." Mindell's theoretical emphasis shifted from focusing on the dream-body link, to focusing on the concept of the "dreaming process" as a unified field.

The world comes knocking

Over time, Mindell shifted his focus to the world outside of one-to-one psychotherapy. Many influences contributed to this, including the creation of the Research Society for Process-oriented Psychology (RS-POP) in 1982. A group of about 50 students, colleagues, and others interested in Mindell's work met and founded a research and training institute. This group quickly found itself dealing with relationship issues, group dynamics, and rank and power. RS-POP itself was an opportunity to test new ideas using a process-oriented approach. Could the dreaming process somehow be used to work with the problems and challenges that arise in relationships, groups, and organizations?

Other factors also contributed to the widening of Mindell's process-oriented approach. Process-oriented Psychology was introduced into social service agencies in and around Zurich, giving it broader public exposure. The publication of Mindell's first books also extended its audience. As Process Work became better known, students came from around the world to study with Mindell in Zurich. Mindell also began to apply Process Work in various settings, and to teach outside Switzerland.

Around this time of expansion and public exposure, Mindell dreamt that the entire globe was his patient.[10] He felt that the problems of the world, the political, social struggles of the planet, and the social context of personal problems, desperately needed attention. Perhaps it was the *Zeitgeist* of the era, or perhaps it was the large group focus that began to develop as more and more people from around the world came to Zurich to study. Whatever the reason, the dream of the "globe as client" was a guiding force in the next ten years of Process Work's evolution. During this era, Process Work expanded into new areas of application, including work with relationships, groups and organizations, and with clients in altered and extreme states of consciousness. It was a "coming out" phase during which Process Work began to interact with other groups and modali-

---

[10] Arnold Mindell, *Sitting in the Fire: Large Group Transformation Using Conflict & Diversity* (Portland, OR: Lao Tse Press, 1995).

ties, communicate to a wider audience, and position itself in the spectrum of psychotherapies.

Three important conceptual developments occurred during this time. Mindell's work with the chronically mentally ill resulted in a theory and method of working with extreme and altered states of consciousness, such as psychoses, comatose states, and addictive processes. His wife, Amy Mindell, made a major contribution to the theory and practice of Process Work with her concept of metaskills,[11] or feeling attitudes, and her description of their role in the practice of Process Work. Increased interaction with the wider community, and a growing emphasis on groups, relationships and social processes, led to the development of Worldwork, a process-oriented approach to group work.

City shadows

In the mid-1980s, Mindell was invited to work with the staff and patients of a mental health agency in Duebendorf, Switzerland.[12] This agency setting included doctors, social workers, patients, interns, and also politicians who were responsible for funding the agency. Mindell worked with patients at the agency, and also with the larger social issue of mental health in the city. He wrote about his work in this area in *City Shadows: Psychological Interventions in Psychiatry,*[13] which connected process concepts to psychiatry. In calling psychiatric patients "city shadows," Mindell emphasized the relativity of psychotic states of consciousness. Rather than use the term "psychosis," Mind-

---

[11] Amy Mindell, *Metaskills: The Spiritual Art of Therapy* (Tempe, AZ: New Falcon Press, 1994. Reprint. Portland, OR: Lao Tse Press, 2003).

[12] Jean-Claude Audergon was working at the agency, and organized Mindell's visit. Audergon subsequently applied Process Work in various mental health settings around the world, helping to establish its presence in the psychiatric community.

[13] Arnold Mindell, *City Shadows: Psychological Interventions in Psychiatry* (New York: Routledge, 1988).

ell coined the term "extreme state" to reflect his observation that the values and norms of a given culture determine whether a state of mind is normal or abnormal. He saw extreme states, such as schizophrenia, catatonia, and depression, in a value-neutral way, as alternative states of experience, rather than as fixed, pathological conditions. His city shadow approach looked for value and meaning in these states of consciousness, and sought ways of making them more useful and less disturbing to individuals and society.

The spiritual art of therapy

A second major conceptual development came about after the Esalen Institute invited Arnold and Amy Mindell to be therapists-in-residence. The Esalen Institute, in California, is an internationally known center for psychotherapy and personal growth. While the Mindells were in residence at Esalen, therapists would ask them to elaborate on their work, and contrast it with other approaches. This prompted Amy Mindell to study her husband's work in greater detail, in order to understand the spiritual attitudes and feeling approaches that lay behind Process Work techniques.[14] Her doctoral dissertation, later published as a book entitled *Metaskills: The Spiritual Art of Therapy*, details metaskills used in Process Work, and discusses their importance for psychotherapy in general. Amy Mindell's work represented a turning point in the development of Process Work. Her introduction of the concept of metaskills made the spiritual dimension of psychotherapeutic practice more explicit.

Working with the world

After spending years traveling to the United States to teach, the Mindells and many of their colleagues moved to Portland, Oregon, to set up a new training and research institute in the United States. Propelled by the desire to apply Process Work to social problems, they hoped that North America would be a

---

[14] Amy Mindell, *Metaskills.*

fertile environment for the next phase of Process Work's development: its social and political application in group and community life.

Mindell introduced his early ideas on group work in his book *The Year I: Global Process Work with Planetary Tensions.*[15] His method of group transformation and conflict resolution, or "group process," was a way for groups to work on their identity, internal conflicts, disturbances, and overall development.[16] Mindell founded his process-oriented approach to groups on the concept of "deep democracy." Deep democracy involves helping the various parts of a group to come forward and interact with each other, including those parts that have been silenced, or seen as disturbing. Out of the interaction between all of these parts, conflicts can be resolved, and a deeper sense of community created.

In the early 1990s, annual "Worldwork" seminars began. These seminars were large international forums, in which the principles and methods of deep democracy were applied to social and political issues. Worldwork methods also began to be used to address social and political tensions in community forums, organizations, and other group settings. In such settings, Mindell and his colleagues saw that members of socially marginalized groups often took the role of "disturber" in a group, raising issues and interacting in ways which were put down or ignored by the group as a whole. This placed responsibility for change on marginalized groups and individuals, when

---

[15] Arnold Mindell, *The Year I: Global Process Work with Planetary Tensions* (New York: Penguin-Arkana, 1989). See also Jan Dworkin, "Group Process: A Stage for Personal and Planetary Growth" (Ph.D. diss., The Union Institute, 1989).

[16] Mindell initially described practical methods of working with group process in his book, *The Leader as Martial Artist: An Introduction to Deep Democracy Techniques and Strategies for Resolving Conflict and Creating Community* (San Francisco: HarperCollins, 1992. Reprint. Portland, OR: Lao Tse Press, 2000).

in fact it was the mainstream tendency to disavow or ignore aspects of its own experience that dreamt up the role of disturber. As a result, Mindell's approach to group work increasingly focused on the dynamics of marginalization, power and rank.

Mindell identified multiple dimensions of power and rank as having an important role in group dynamics. These included psychological and spiritual rank (inner strengths such as self-esteem, ease in conflict, and spiritual beliefs), as well as socio-cultural status (based on a person's social and material circumstances). His concept of deep democracy expanded to include the disavowed dreaming experiences of individuals, as well as the marginalized parts of a group. Deep democracy was not only a socio-political method of addressing conflict and other social issues, but also a spiritual and psychological awareness method, which enabled people to find fluidity and wholeness in the midst of social tensions.

Mindell was concerned that group participants in the heat of conflict were often held in the grip of their social identity. The reality of injustice and heat of emotions tended to obscure the dreaming dimensions of interactions. Mindell sought to develop group work methods that did not privilege social issues over dreaming experiences. He wanted deep democracy to be an inner experience, as well as a social encounter. He questioned how people might use their awareness and access their inner diversity, even in the midst of social tension and injustice. How might they remember transcendent realities while in the grip of an urgent social issue? To find answers to these questions, Mindell dug deeper into the nature of consciousness and reality, and the role of awareness in conflict. He returned to his early studies of mathematics and physics, hoping to find out more about the "mystery that lies behind our human form."[17]

---

[17] Arnold Mindell, *Quantum Mind*, 13.

Towards a sentient psychology

The years that Mindell spent exploring the connection between physics and psychology brought him full circle to his earliest studies at the Jung Institute. While he was a student, he had attempted to bridge the material world of physics and the psychological world of thoughts, feelings, and unconscious experience through his studies of synchronicity. Later, as an analyst, he experimented with the mind-body connection. Then, 30 years after first trying to bridge psychology and physics, he returned to physics, this time seeking the theoretical connection that linked the material world to dreaming reality.

Mindell was motivated by his experience of working as a psychotherapist for over three decades, which showed him how people everywhere seemed to suffer from being cut off from their dreaming experiences, no matter what their presenting problem or diagnosis. He believed that "[i]gnoring the Dreaming is an undiagnosed global epidemic. People suffer from a chronic form of mild depression when they are taught to focus on everyday reality and forget about the Dreaming background."[18] Wherever he worked, Mindell saw that suffering came not only from social problems, inequity and injustice, but also from treading too lightly on the surface of existence, from an inability to connect to non-ordinary reality.

From the late 1990s, Mindell extended his theory of dreaming to take into account a dream-like reality that permeates everything. He called this the "Dreaming,"[19] or the sentient essence level of reality. Mindell differentiated this level of reality from the two other levels he had addressed in his earlier work: "consensus reality" (the everyday world of time and space that is generally agreed upon as "real" and is perceived

---

[18] Arnold Mindell, *Dreaming While Awake. Techniques for 24-hour Lucid Dreaming* (Charlottesville, VA: Hampton Roads, 2000), 7.

[19] "Dreaming," capitalized, is used to denote the realm of undifferentiated experience, what Mindell also calls sentient reality. The smaller case "dreaming" refers to noticing and following dream-like experiences.

through everyday awareness), and "Dreamland" (the world of the dreams, projections, emotions, fantasies, and the like). Acknowledging the influence of ancient indigenous traditions and contemporary physicists, Mindell explained the "Dreaming" as a sentient reality beneath the threshold of awareness, an unbroken wholeness, out of which signals, dreams, and all other experiential phenomena arise.

Mindell described this understanding of reality and its relationship to dreamwork in *Dreaming While Awake*. He also published a theoretical exploration of the background that unifies physics and psychology, *Quantum Mind*. Following these conceptual breakthroughs, Mindell began to apply sentient work, as he called it, to dream and bodywork, and to worldwork. He developed sentient methods that helped people glimpse this non-dualistic level of reality, and bring insights and expanded perspectives back to the everyday world of conflict and problems. He discovered that sentient work had a profoundly healing effect on individuals, large groups, and even conflict situations. [20]

Mindell's sentient approach to psychology contributes to a paradigm shift away from western psychology's emphasis on the individual psyche. While the last hundred years of western psychology has centered on personality development, behavioral problems, and helping people develop a sense of identity, sentient psychology focuses on helping people to drop their sense of self, become more aware of the way in which they separate themselves from the "other," and develop a more fluid and multifaceted identity. When Mindell first described deep

---

[20] Mindell's recent research extends Taoism's concept of "the Way" to include the paths and possibilities of elementary particle physics. His recent re-explorations (2002-2005) of Richard Feynman's *QED* (Princeton, NJ: Princeton University Press, 1985), will soon be published. These new ideas connect Taoism, quantum physics, and the sentient directional consciousness of Aboriginal peoples, making it possible to discover new meanings to dreams and feelings.

democracy, he contrasted it to regular democracy by recalling its etymological origin. *Demokratie*, he wrote, comes from the Greek *demos*, meaning people, and *kratie*, meaning power. Through his work on sentience, Mindell saw that regular democracy is about power, but deep democracy is about awareness. Sentient psychology gave him the key he was looking for in working towards deep democracy. Sentient methods help people use their awareness to step outside their everyday identity, and identify with the wider whole.

From Mindell's early research into mind-body phenomena in the late 1970s, to his work on sentience in the early to mid 2000s, the development of Process Work has encompassed various areas: body work, community and large group work, conflict resolution, addiction work, relationship work, coma work, and work with altered and extreme states. It has been influenced by, and has contributed to, a range of traditions and disciplines, including shamanism, consciousness studies, medicine and alternative healing traditions, psychology, psychiatry, and physics. As Process Work moves into its fourth decade of development, it is no longer predominantly a psychotherapeutic modality. Due to its increased focus on sentience, it may be described more accurately as an awareness discipline, with applications across a variety of domains.

The thread that has held the development of Process Work together as a coherent body of theory and practice is Mindell's recognition of a background dreaming reality to everyday life and its problems. His original theory of the Dreambody, and the techniques he developed for following dreaming phenomena, have greatly diversified, but the basic principles of Process Work remain close to their origins. The next chapter introduces these key principles and the remainder of the book illustrates how to apply them in practice.

Chapter 2

Basic Concepts in Process Work

To go along with Nature effortlessly, as does a fish or a master artisan, is to swim with the current, to let one's knife slip along with the grain. When nature is taken as a guide, a friend, living becomes almost effortless, tranquil, joyous even. Care departs; serenity takes over.   *John Blofeld* [21]

Practicing Process Work involves understanding "process" as the flow of experience in oneself and in the environment, and following this flow in a differentiated way. The Taoist masters taught that aligning oneself to nature or "the Tao" as it changes is the key to a balanced and happy life. Resisting change or struggling against the Tao creates tensions and difficulties. Transformation occurs naturally once a person is able to

---

[21] John Blofeld, *Taoism: The Road to Immortality* (Boulder, CO: Shambhala,1978),10.

trust nature, and go along with what is happening. Of course, this is easier said than done! The ancient Taoists developed their own system of following process, as have other traditions. Process Work offers a conceptual and practical system of following process in contemporary life, building on foundational Taoist ideas with concepts and techniques influenced by psychology, physics and various spiritual traditions. In this chapter, we will introduce some of these basic concepts, in preparation for the detailed description of practicing Process Work that follows in the remainder of the book.

Following the flow of process

Following the flow of process involves "caring for the absurd and impossible," and going against conventional beliefs and ways of seeing things. Using a metaphor from the Native American tradition, Mindell says that following a process is like "riding the horse backwards." It requires a different way of seeing. "Following the unwanted, unintended message goes against collective belief, which says that if you follow the unknown, it will lead you off the edge of the world. ... But process work shows the roundness of our universe. It shows that if we have the courage to follow unintentional signals...we do not fall off, but discover new worlds."[22] Looking into our dreams, noticing whether or not we feel inclined in a certain direction, flipping a coin, checking in with our body energy, and other means of tapping awareness and information outside of rational thought, are all ways of following process.

Following the flow of process also involves going with what is happening in a given moment, rather than resisting it. This does not mean just letting things happen, or passively accepting oppression or harm. It means that when an obstacle or difficulty arises, we face it in order to find out what changes

---

[22] Arnold Mindell with Amy Mindell, *Riding the Horse Backwards: Process Work in Theory and Practice*, 11.

are meant for us in that challenge. This is a spiritual attitude, one that is interested in discovering how our innermost being attunes itself to whatever arises in everyday life, and how this prevents us from being victimized by our experiences.

At first, following process by turning in the direction of oncoming trouble may feel counter-intuitive, or even dangerous. As any novice skier discovers, turning one's skis downhill is the best way to gain control of the skis, although this feels counter-intuitive at first. The skier fears that pointing her skis down the slope will make her go too fast and lose control, until she finds out that by doing so, she is better able to navigate the mountain's challenging terrain. Going with the Tao by turning to face oncoming troubles frees us up, because physical and emotional energy are no longer spent in resistance. Like the downhill skier, we find we are able to enjoy the ride and respond with greater ease and flexibility to whatever comes.

Differentiating the flow of process

In his early work, Mindell describes process as "the change in what we observe, the flow of signals and the messages they carry."[23] Differentiating the flow of process involves noticing change as it occurs and the elusive or hidden dimensions of experience. Process Work initially differentiated the flow of process in terms of "primary process" and "secondary process"[24] separated by an "edge." Later, the concepts of consensus reality, nonconsensus reality and marginalization became used more frequently, giving greater emphasis to the role of awareness in following a process.

---

[23] Ibid, 9–10.

[24] Mindell's use of this terminology is opposite to Freud's labelling of the structure of the psyche. Freud used the term "primary" (meaning primal or less revised by consciousness) to refer to the unconscious, instinctual material of the Id. He used the term "secondary" for the contents of consciousness that had undergone a process of revision or reconsideration, and were more acceptable to the ego.

Primary process, secondary process and the edge

Primary process refers to those experiences that are better known and closer to a person's sense of identity. Secondary process refers to those experiences that are further from a person's sense of identity. Primary and secondary processes are separated by an "edge." The edge represents the limit of the known identity, as well as a point of contact with unknown experiences or identities. An edge is often felt as discomfort, nervousness or excitement because it is an encounter with something new or unfamiliar.

The concepts of primary and secondary process and the edge offer a conceptual framework for tracking experience and organizing perceptual information. This framework is helpful for discerning which parts of a person's experience are closer to his everyday sense of himself, and which parts are split off and hold potentially useful meaning and information for his normal identity. In everyday life, we constantly receive messages from the primary and secondary process, in ourselves and from other people. Primary and secondary information often contradict or conflict with each other. For example, a worker might complain to her colleagues that she feels exhausted, but spend an hour chatting animatedly on the phone to a friend. A man might come out of his apartment smiling cheerily at his neighbor, while turning away and hurrying to get down the hall quickly before he gets trapped in a long conversation. And who has not had the experience of saying or doing something that they never intended?

Processes are rarely completely known (primary) or unknown (secondary). Some appear only as remote and murky dream images, while others are well known (primary), but disliked or judged (secondary). A person may be aware of a secondary process, but be unable to see its value. This can be seen in the following example of a facilitator, "Laura," working with a woman who has a meditative tendency that pulls her towards introversion. The client, "Jean," is a busy person, who is engaged and successful at work and has a lively, growing family.

Her primary process description of herself is "busy," "active," and "nurturing." Introversion is a secondary process for her. She is aware of this tendency, but experiences it as "depressing." She dislikes it and cannot see that it has any value in her life. She wishes it would just disappear. Jean's primary process of activity and her secondary process of inwardness are separated by an edge. This edge is structured by Jean's belief that she does not have time for meditation, which she does not see as valuable. In Laura's work with Jean, the concepts of "primary," "secondary," and "edge," serve as an interactive, dynamic schema to differentiate the various parts of Jean's process, pointing to experiences that might need to find fuller expression in Jean's life.

Consensus and nonconsensus realms and marginalization

As Process Work has developed, other terms have come into use to describe the flow of process. While "primary process," "secondary process," and "the edge" are still used to describe and track the flow of an individual's experience, the broader concepts of consensus reality, nonconsensus reality, and marginalization are additionally used to explain the interplay between perception and experience more fully. Consensus reality (CR) describes the realm of experience that is generally consented to or agreed upon as "real." CR corresponds to majority views and statistical norms. It is a collective understanding about the nature of reality. Nonconsensus reality (NCR) consists of subjective, dream-like experiences that are not generally consented upon as "real," such as dreams, feelings, fantasies, and projections, and other experiences that make up our inner world. While CR experiences can be discussed and described objectively, NCR experiences are those that people do not normally permit themselves to feel, talk about, or notice.

NCR experiences are often marginalized. They may be disavowed, avoided, ignored or simply not noticed. Perception and awareness are governed by marginalization. We cannot function if we do not marginalize certain perceptions in favor of others. At the social level, some experiences are viewed as "normal," and included in our everyday identity and world-view. Others are pushed aside or rejected as "not me." Sometimes experiences are marginalized because they are threatening. Sometimes, this happens when experiences are too subtle or unusual for our ordinary awareness to perceive them. Training in awareness is needed to develop the "lucidity" or "second attention"[25] necessary to perceive such experiences. In all cases, edges are the product of marginalization. They mark the limits of what is perceived, experienced, agreed upon as "real," or incorporated into a person's identity.

In the above example, Jean's CR experience consists of work, family, and all the activities that are part of her busy life. Jean is pestered by her NCR experience of being pulled towards a quieter, more meditative state. She describes her experience of this tendency as a feeling of depression, which comes and goes fleetingly. She describes these feelings to Laura with irritation in her voice, sounding as if she wishes they would go away. Jean's description suggests that the experience is marginalized. Her primary process of activity and belief that meditation is a waste of time casts her introversive tendency in a problem light. Laura uses the concepts of CR, NCR and marginalization to understand Jean's experience more fully. She sees that the CR perspective dominates, and that the NCR experience is neither fully known nor appreciated. As in gossip, a story is being told from one point of view, the CR perspective. Once the NCR and CR components of Jean's experience are identified, she can to get to know her tendencies toward activity and introversion more fully.

---

[25] Arnold Mindell, *The Shaman's Body: A New Shamanism for Transforming Health, Relationships, and Community* (San Francisco: HarperCollins, 1993), 23.

Noticing and unfolding a process

Noticing a process involves the use of differentiated awareness. Borrowing from Carlos Castenada's writings, Mindell used the terms "first attention" and "second attention" to distinguish between different types of awareness and their relationship to consensus and non-consensus realities. First attention is the awareness used to perceive consensus reality world of objects, people, and events. Second attention perceives the unintended, often irrational experiences that are ignored by first attention. Mindell defines second attention as the ability to "[focus] upon things you normally neglect, upon external and internal, subjective, irrational experiences. The second attention is the key to the world of dreaming, the unconscious and dreamlike movements, the accidents, [synchronicities] and slips of the tongue that happen all day long.[26]

Unfolding a process involves noticing a secondary or NCR experience in the initial description of a problem, amplifying its expression until a new meaning or aspect of identity emerges, and then integrating the new experience into everyday life. Process Work employs a detailed method of tracking NCR experience in unfolding a process. This method rests on concepts from communication theory[27] such as intended and unintended communication. The primary process conveys intended communication through language and deliberate gestures. The secondary process conveys unintended communication nonverbally in body posture, gestures, and movements, in speech patterns that hold implicit meaning, and in paralanguage (including tone of voice, rhythm, volume). Ordinary conversation always contains both intended and unintended communication. Confusion and miscommunication in conversation are

---

[26] Ibid, 24–25.

[27] Paul Watzlawick, Janet B. Bavelas, and Don D. Jackson, *The Pragmatics of Human Communication: A Study of Interactional Patterns, Pathologies, and Paradoxes* (London: Faber, 1968).

often the result of double messages, or a mix of intended and unintended communication. Much conflict stems from powerful non-verbal messages that underlie intended communication.

Signals, Channels and Feedback

Intended and unintended communication consists of numerous "signals," or pieces of information. Signals may be easily perceptible or hard to detect. Those that are perceptible to the senses are called "non-flickering" or steady signals because they persist long enough for perception to occur. Signals that barely cross the threshold of perception are called "flickering" signals, "flirts" or "pre-signals."[28] These signals can be noticed fleetingly, but they do not persist long enough or strongly enough to be objects of focus.

The practice of Process Work is based on an ability to detect flickering and non-flickering signals, differentiate between consensus and nonconsensus reality signals, and follow the dreaming signals that lead to the unknown. These dreaming signals lead from consensus reality to dreaming reality. Like stepping-stones in a river, they must be followed precisely, one leading to another. Instead of looking at the far bank, anticipating where we will end up, we need to look for the stone that is immediately in front of us, until we get to the other side.

The tiny bits of dreaming information that appear in flickering and non-flickering signals are collectively referred to as "sensory-grounded information." Sensory-grounded information is the language of the dreaming process. It communicates secondary information on its own terms and in its own way. Normally, secondary process is described through the filter of the primary process's ideas and interpretations. For instance, Jean's meditative tendency is described by her primary process as a problematic feeling of depression. This is not a description of the dreaming experience itself. In order to find out about the dreaming experience on its own terms, free of primary process

---

[28] Arnold Mindell, *Dreaming While Awake.*

bias, sensory-grounded information must be elicited. To do so, Laura asks Jean to describe her feeling of depression. She asks, "How do you experience the depression?" Laura replies that it feels like something pulling her inwards, making her feel "heavy," and "low." As she speaks, she looks down, and her eyes close slightly. Her breathing becomes slow, and her shoulders sag slightly. These verbal, paralinguistic and non-verbal signals are all sensory-grounded information. They are stepping-stones to the dreaming process hidden in Jean's experience of depression.

Sensory-grounded signals are communicated through "channels." A channel is a sensory, motor or relational mode of perceiving or communicating experience. When we look at or see something we are using the visual channel. Feeling something in the body happens in the proprioceptive channel. Experiencing something through movement occupies the kinesthetic channel, and hearing something or using sound to communicate engages the auditory channel. We also have experiences in the relationship channel, in interaction with others, or in the world channel, in which experience is centered in the environment (for example, institutions, world events, the earth, nature). Returning to the example of Jean's work with Laura, the signals of Jean's secondary process of introversion (sighing, sagging, eyes slightly closed) are mainly communicated in the proprioceptive channel. This is also conveyed in Jean's first description of her experience as a body sensation, using words like "heavy" and "low." If Jean had said she felt "pulled" or "pressed down," then she would be using movement or kinesthetic words to express the secondary experience. The channel or channels though which her dreaming signals are conveyed indicate the most effective way of establishing communication with a dreaming process.

Feedback and amplification

Following sensory-grounded information is governed by "feedback." Process Work adopted the concept of feedback from systems thinking. In systems thinking, feedback is information that helps to adjust or maintain a system's output. It may be negative or positive. A thermostat in a home heating system is a good example of a feedback system. The thermostat receives information on the temperature of the home. If the information it receives is "negative," or different than the current temperature setting, the thermostat turns on the furnace to increase heat output, or turns off the furnace to reduce the heat output. Feedback enables the system to remain in a stable state (homeostasis), without escalating out of control or running down.

Although Process Work borrowed the terms "negative feedback" and "positive feedback" from systems thinking, it uses them somewhat differently. "Positive feedback" refers to the strengthening of a signal in response to an intervention. "Negative feedback" refers to a lack of noticeable increase in the strength of a signal in response to an intervention. Negative feedback does not mean that an intervention is "wrong," and positive feedback does not indicate that an intervention is "right." Both negative and positive feedback provide information about a person's process, pointing to the next stepping-stone in the process of accessing dreaming experience.

Returning to the above example, Laura's question about Jean's depressed feeling is an intervention that elicits more information about Jean's secondary process. When Laura asks, "How do you experience the depression?" Jean's shoulders droop and her eyes close slightly, as she describes the heavy, low feeling that comes over her. This increase in the output of dreaming signals is positive feedback. It tells Laura that the dreaming process feels addressed and is communicating itself in its own language. Jean's non-verbal signals are a "somatic reply" to Laura's intervention, a physical response that suggests willingness to go more deeply into an internal state.

When signals are "spoken to," through a therapist's attention and encouragement, they increase their strength or "self-amplify." Like a person who is lost in the woods, dreaming signals shout to be heard. If they get no response, their voices get weaker. When they finally hear someone calling them, they get excited! Someone is out there! Their shouts grow stronger again. Amplifying sensory-grounded signals by following feedback allows a dreaming experience to emerge.

Double signals and dreaming up

Most signal exchanges happen below the threshold of ordinary awareness. Even though we may notice some of the non-verbal signals of the secondary process, a special kind of awareness is needed to follow and unfold them, and to understand their message. Without the ability to distinguish between primary and secondary signals, we may become confused or irritated by double messages. For instance, Jean's non-verbal signals communicate depression, while her verbal signals communicate how busy, upbeat, and active she is. Her introversion is communicated through subtle non-verbal signals of drooping shoulders, half closed eyes, and trailing-off sentences.

Double messages, or "double signals" as they are called in Process Work terms, can result in a phenomenon called "dreaming up." Dreaming up refers to the effect of one person's unintended communication on another. Someone is dreamed up when they respond to another person's unintended communication signals without being aware of the communication that has triggered their response. Dreaming up happens as a normal part of all human interaction. It can happen between friends, family members, acquaintances, as well as between facilitator and client.[29] Here is an everyday example of dreaming up. Two friends are engaged in a conversation, and one of them does not notice the subtle signals of tension in the other's body posture, facial expression, and tone of voice. He begins to react to his friend's signals by withdrawing a little,

---

[29] For a comprehensive exploration of dreaming up, its theory and therapeutic uses, see Joseph Goodbread, *Radical Intercourse, How Dreams Unite Us in Love, Conflict and Other Inevitable Relationships* (Portland, OR: Lao Tse Press), 1997.

feeling that his friend is unhappy with him in some way. All of this happens outside of his awareness. His reactions just happen to him. Once he is no longer in his friend's company, these reactions disappear. This is also a characteristic of dreamed up experience. The experience only persists as long as someone is in the presence of another person's double signals.

Who is following the process?

Following a process depends on the awareness of both client and facilitator. The facilitator differentiates primary from secondary process, noticing signals, channels, and perceiving subtle feedback. This requires the development of a subtle awareness that perceives NCR experiences. The client becomes aware of her experience, notices what she senses, feels, and perceives, and tunes into experiences that are far from her everyday identity. For this reason, Process Work is often referred to as an awareness method. In particular, noticing experience outside everyday consciousness requires a detached awareness, which is commonly referred to as the "metacommunicator."

The metacommunicator

So far our discussion of following a process has focused on differentiating between the primary (CR) and secondary (NCR) parts of a process. This involves distinguishing between those characteristics that a person views as "me," and those that are experienced as "other" or disturbing in some way. Another important task in following a process is to become aware of the narrator of an experience. In other words, it is important to be able to discern *who* is telling the story.

How a person describes their process is a function of the *metacommunicator*. The metacommunicator is similar to the concept of the "detached observer" found in Buddhism. It is a self-reflective capacity to notice, organize, and report on one's experiences. Sometimes it is also called a "witness," "observer," "narrator," or "inner facilitator." The metacommunicator becomes evident through listening closely to how people talk about their experiences, and asking oneself, "Who is telling the story here?" "Who is reporting on this problem, and how are they describing it?" If a person says "I shouldn't be so angry, but I can't help it," she is not only telling you her problem (anger) but is also telling you what her metacommunicator thinks about it (it shouldn't be so strong).

If we have not actively cultivated the capacity for detached awareness, our perception of our process is not neutral. Conditioned ways of looking at the world, ourselves, and our problems filter our perceptual experience. Upbringing, education, cultural influences, religious beliefs, worldviews, and personal history color our perceptions. As a result, the metacommunicator is often biased. It disavows secondary experiences, such as dreamfigures, by organizing awareness through the filter of the primary process. The following example of a writer at work illustrates this. The writer is working on the task of completing a book. He becomes aware of a back pain from sitting too long in one spot. As soon as he notices the pain, he becomes irritated and thinks: "Oh no! My back hurts, but I am almost finished, I don't what to stop." His metacommunicator, the one who notices his backache, is aligned with his task of writing the book. It is noticing his experience but has a bias in the direction of his primary process goals (see Figure 2.1).

The process of reflecting on and working with inner experiences, whether through specific psychological or meditative practices, or through general life experience, changes the stance of the metacommunicator. Gradually, our perception becomes more neutral and the metacommunicator is no longer filtered through the biases and judgments of everyday consciousness. The metacommunicator becomes more interested in the whole than in one particular part. In a sense, a developed metacommunicator is deeply democratic, like a good group facilitator. It looks out for parts of the personality that have been left out or

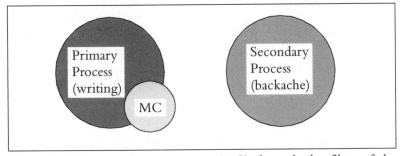

Figure 2.1 The metacommunicator (MC) through the filter of the primary process

ignored, and makes space for them to come forward, express themselves, and interact with other parts.

A developed and more neutral metacommunicator is also called second attention. It has the capacity to notice NCR experiences as well as CR phenomena. Second attention has a greater capacity for self-reflection than everyday awareness. It distinguishes between perceptions of sensory experience and judgments about that experience, and is therefore vital in following a dreaming process. Without the ability to distinguish perception from judgment and interpretation, it is easy to get lost in reaction to an experience and be unable to enter the dreaming experience itself. In the example of the writer, he becomes aware of a slight back pain from sitting too long in one spot. As soon as he notices the pain, he becomes aware of a vague feeling of irritation, and the thought: "I don't want to have to move! I want to finish this before the end of the morning." His capacity for detached metacommunication serves to differentiate between his various perceptions, without aligning itself with any of them. Although one experience (his irritation) is antagonistic to another (his backache), his second attention does not align itself with either of these experiences. Instead, it regards them both with a kind of neutral curiosity. This is represented in Figure 2.2.

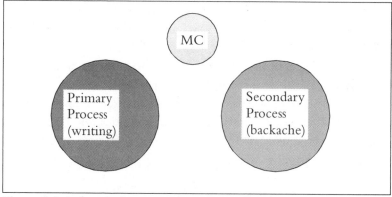

Figure 2.2 A detached metacommunicator (MC)

The metacommunication continuum

The capacity to metacommunicate can be thought of as a continuum. At one end of the metacommunication continuum are states of awareness that allow a person to reflect, track, and communicate about his experience. At the other end of the continuum are states of consciousness, such as psychotic and comatose states, in which there is little or no metacommunicative capacity. Between the two furthest poles on the continuum lie other states of consciousness, characterized by varying capacities to think and talk neutrally about personal experience. For example, a person in a strong affect, such as anger or sadness, might be unable to talk about her experience for moments at a time. The capacity to metacommunicate is momentarily slightly diminished. More strongly altered states, which last long enough to threaten everyday functioning, have a more reduced metacommunicator.

For instance, if someone is in an altered state, they may not be able to talk normally. If you ask someone, "How are you today?" and the person goes into a long period of withdrawal, interventions that rely on the person's capacity to metacommunicate will not work. Instead, interventions that do not engage the person's everyday consciousness are needed. The facilitator could join the person's state, sitting quietly with them, or, focusing on her own inner experience, she could follow her own withdrawing tendencies, whatever they may be. Or, the facilitator could speak aloud, without talking directly to the client, about the situation, her inner conflict about withdrawal or socially engaging. If it is appropriate for the situation and person, the facilitator can change channels, and encourage the client's withdrawn state by using movement, or touch. However she works, the facilitator must use an intervention that follows the person's process without using the filter of the metacommunicator.

A detached metacommunicator can be difficult to access even when a person is in a so-called normal state of consciousness. For instance, whenever we are in a mood, such as hurt, sulking, angry, or jealous, it often feels impossible to reflect neutrally on these feelings. The metacommunicator itself is submerged in the mood. Process Work with moods, affects, and with extreme or altered states of consciousness, uses methods for accessing secondary processes without relying on interventions that use normal metacommunication.

Metaskills

The neutrality and detachment of the facilitator reflect her developed metacommunicator or second attention, and also her metaskills.[30] Metaskills are the feeling attitudes, values and beliefs that deeply inform our way of working with others. Metaskills encompass beliefs about life and death, nature, learning and growth, as well as the feeling with which skills are applied. They breathe life into interventions, making them effective, making our work come alive.

Metaskills are "grown" rather than learned. They may develop naturally out of life experience, or they may develop as a result of conscious effort. Many metaskills come naturally to people, sometimes from an early age. Others come from grow-

---

[30] Amy Mindell, *Metaskills*.

ing older or undergoing hardship. Some people develop metaskills in association with an intentional life path or spiritual practice, or through the influence of a teacher or mentor. Others develop them through their work in the world or in their relationships with other people. Some of the metaskills that are central to the practice of Process Work are described below.

Following nature

"Following nature" involves trusting that a solution or way forward will emerge out of our dreams. This approach is fundamental to the practice of Process Work. Trusting nature, and trusting the process, means that the real facilitator of a process is nature, not a person. The metaskill of following nature is:

> [the] loving attitude which supports that which is trying to happen. She is that regal attitude which gives up one's own way in order to amplify the supraordination of fate. ... [She possesses a special] relationship to the world of nature and its happenings and can follow them even when their direction seems foreign.[31]

When the facilitator trusts nature, he is open to and respects the dreaming process. He has a sincere desire to observe its signals and follow them exactly. He views his task as facilitating a relationship between the conscious identity and the dreaming process, which seeks expression through difficulties or disturbances.[32] Problem solving or healing is not his goal, although they may happen as part of the process. Trusting nature also means believing in the client, and believing that the client's process will show the way. Under the healing influence of this metaskill, clients do not feel pathologized, and feel less

---

[31] Arnold Mindell, *River's Way: The Process Science of the Dreambody* (London, England: Routledge & Kegan Paul, 1985) 137-38.

[32] While this concept of facilitator is found in many written and oral teachings of Process Work, we are indebted to Max Schupbach for his particular emphasis on therapist as "inner relationship facilitator."

pressure to change or get somewhere. Following nature also benefits facilitators, since the facilitator who follows nature is less prone to burn out because she does not resist what is happening. Instead of straining to bring about change or come up with a solution, she follows the wisdom of the process, and the solutions that brings.

Beginner's mind

"Beginner's mind" means following a process without judgment, interpretation, or bias. A beginner's mind is curious, open, and eager. It does not look at life with a jaundiced or skeptical eye. It views every experience as something new. Walking in the woods often teaches beginner's mind. Even if we walk the same trail, each day there is something fresh, new and unexpected. A bud on a tree is there this morning, but was not there yesterday. Mushrooms sprout overnight and if we are still thinking of yesterday's walk, we will miss seeing the new crop of golden chanterelle mushrooms peeking out from under the pine needles.

Using a beginner's mind, the facilitator notices the bare bones of an experience, its most basic structure. If a client speaks about being hurt by her partner's aloof nature, the facilitator hears the story as if she has no idea what "hurt," "partner" or "aloof" mean. Everything needs to be approached with an empty mind, as if there were no prior knowledge of that experience. If the facilitator thinks "hurt" means sad and feeling abandoned, she might miss the little twinkle in the client's eye when she talks about the partner's aloof nature. She might miss the extra emphasis and dreamy look in how the client describes the partner, and miss a doorway into something special. She will assume that the process is about being hurt and feeling abandoned, but miss an opportunity to explore the client's fascination with her own possible aloofness and detachment.

The facilitator with a beginner's mind is curious, and delights in learning and exploring nature. Like a visitor in a new world, she takes in fresh information, respects it, and learns from it. Without this metaskill, facilitators struggle to follow their clients' experiences accurately. They may miss the signals of the dreaming process, because they are too preoccupied with judging, guiding, or interpreting the process from their own viewpoint.

Eldership

An elder is like a loving grandmother who makes you feel better, but has seen too much and done too much to get all wrapped up in the particulars and passions of everyday life. The metaskill of eldership is an attitude of support and love, and above all, inclusiveness. It values every part of a person's process, and seeks to facilitate the expression of all the parts. The elder does not push for outcomes. She does not work hard towards a particular goal. She embraces a client's goal, but also sees more than the momentary situation. This attitude is not an easy one to develop. Compassion for people and wanting the best for others often makes us join our clients in pushing for things to change. Even though this may be helpful, it is only one part of a client's process. The metaskill of eldership sees things from a long-term perspective, and recognizes the momentary and the eternal, the personal and the impersonal.

The elder is capable of working at different levels of reality simultaneously, and can follow a process in the present moment, while keeping in mind a sense of history and context. The authority of the elder derives from this comprehensive viewpoint, and a sense of being guided by something greater than himself. This metaskill generates trust, because it is impartial and unattached to any particular outcome.

No change

Barbara Hannah, one of Mindell's favorite teachers, used to say that if a person wanted to change, he needs two things. He has to really want to change, and must also love himself exactly as he is! Change is most likely when we are also really happy with ourselves. "No change" is the metaskill of knowing that there is nothing to do, and that everything is fine the way it is. Change and no change are equally desirable. There is a Zen Buddhist saying, "every day is a fine day." This saying illustrates the attitude of the no change metaskill. No effort is needed. Everything is perfect, even when we hate it!

The no change metaskill rests on the belief that sustainable change happens only with the consent of all parts. If change occurs by devaluing one state and throwing it out in favor of another, the part that has been thrown out may come back to assert itself and sabotage what has already been accomplished. People often try to quit harmful addictions in a fit of anger and disgust. Motivated by this, they vow to kick the habit, but often slip back into the addiction after a while. Like revolutions in which one regime changes for another, the change does not run deep. It works for a while, but real change cannot be effected by hating one particular part. It grows out of a deep acceptance and understanding of all parts, even as we may want to change some of them.

You today, me tomorrow

"You today, me tomorrow" is the kind of compassion that comes from realizing that at any time, we may find ourselves in another's shoes. It is simple, common sense that reminds us that we are not immune from life's problems. We are all in the same boat. This type of compassion is more than an empathetic appreciation of others' experience, or even sympathy for the troubles that befall them. It recognizes the mysterious workings of fate, and acknowledges that the ups and downs of life happen to everyone. In therapeutic settings, clients can sense when facilitators hold themselves apart from the process, and can feel put down by this. They tend to feel less lonely and more able to face difficulties and the unknown when approached with the affiliative metaskill of "you today, me tomorrow".

In this chapter we have introduced some of the main theoretical concepts behind the practice of Process Work. The focus of the next chapter shifts from theory to practice, in introducing thinking skills, feeling attitudes, and techniques useful for observing, mapping, and intervening in the flow of process.

Chapter 3

Mapping the Process

Following a process is an invitation to travel somewhere you have never been, to embrace possibility and have an experience that changes your life. How does a person set out on such a path? What kind of map is useful, or even possible, when no path exists? This chapter introduces "process structure" as a way of mapping the untrodden path of an unfolding process. It explores ways of thinking, metaskills, perceptual skills, and practical techniques that are useful in the early stages of following a process.

Process structure is a self-generating, fluid framework that enables a facilitator to unfold a process by identifying its various emergent parts, particularly those which serve as "dream doors," or ways of engaging with and going deeply into a dreaming process. This framework is constructed out of the interaction between facilitator and client. By noticing the client's verbal and nonverbal communication signals carefully, the facilitator gains a sense of the various parts of a process, and their relationship to one another in an overall network of parts. Some parts appear more "mainstream," or closer to the client's primary identity. Others appear more "marginalized," or further from the client's primary identity. As a process unfolds, this relationship changes. Marginalized experience is made more focal and explored in greater detail and depth, opening up new worlds of experience.

Thinking skills in mapping a process

Process structure is not a fixed plan, but a dynamic, often unpredictable framework. It is like the kind of map that is featured in fairytales, where signposts change direction, roads appear and disappear, destinations change, and strange or marvelous creatures pop up. To allow a process structure to emerge, a facilitator interacts with what her client says about the experience, and with the ways it is revealed in non-verbal behavior. She asks questions to obtain a sense of the client's experience. She makes initial guesses about which parts of the flow of information are primary, which parts are secondary, and possible edges that lie between them. Each piece of information helps to identify a pattern of parts and their interrelationship, which is confirmed or discarded at each step by the next piece of information that emerges. Building a process structure is an iterative process. It occurs not once, but many times, in cycles that build on one another. Hypotheses and questions are formed, discarded, reformed, and elaborated based on the client's feedback.

Inductive thinking

Mapping a process uses a special kind of thinking, known as inductive reasoning. Using this kind of thinking, little bits of information are pieced together, and a model is constructed from fragmentary pieces of data. The only way to check on the usefulness of the model as it evolves is to see if it holds up in relation to new pieces of information, and if it continues to generate further information and energy.

Inductive thinking is used in many areas of everyday life. Detectives use inductive thinking when they piece together clues, alibis, and motives to construct a model of a crime. Poker players also use this type of thinking. With each new card revealed, a new picture of the cards an opponent might hold is formed and the previous picture is discarded. People also use inductive thinking whenever they are in a new situation, or encountering something they have never done before. In such situations, they have no prior knowledge, nothing to fall back on, no guidebook or manual to tell them what is what and how to do things. For instance, a person who travels to a foreign country and does not speak the local language or know the customs of the place, must scan the new environment, trying to construct models of what is happening, what people are saying, how things work, in order to begin to participate and interact. Using inductive reasoning, a person will "try to fill in the gaps on the fly by forming hypotheses, by making analogies, by drawing from past experience, by using heuristic rules of thumb."[33]

Inductive reasoning resembles an evolutionary style of learning and adapting to conditions in the environment. Thrown into an unknown environment, people must construct models of the mystery around them. They are not concerned with whether their model is true or accurate, but with whether it works, whether it helps them survive. This way of thinking has also been called "parallel thinking".[34] Defined briefly, parallel thinking means exploring a given space of possibilities. It involves building a model based on possibilities, exploration,

---

[33] Mitchell Waldrop, *Complexity: The Emerging Science at the Edge of Order and Chaos.* (New York: Touchstone, 1992), 253.

[34] Edward de Bono, *Parallel Thinking: From Socratic to De Bono Thinking* (London: Penguin), 1994.

perception, guessing, and imagination, rather than deciding on a right or wrong move.

In order to work with process structure, these ways of thinking are useful. They help create a map of a process structure as it emerges. They are not concerned with correctness or solutions, but with the overall layout of the process. If a particular guess turns out to be wrong, or confusion sets in, there is no need to go back the beginning of the process structure and start again. The facilitator can simply make another guess based on the information available, send out new exploratory tentacles, and see what comes next, looking for a way forward to reveal itself.

Not knowing

Psychotherapy practitioners often feel subject to the pressure to know and to be wise when working with clients. However, in mapping a process structure, a Process Work facilitator is best served by the metaskill of beginner's mind, which allows the facilitator to be comfortable with not knowing, and be open to guidance from a client's direct or indirect feedback. A momentary process structure needs to be checked against the client's feedback and adjusted as the work proceeds. The pressure to know and "get it right" interferes with the facilitator's ability to do this. It moves the facilitator away from a "bare bones" perception of signals, towards interpretation and problem solving. The facilitator does not have to ask the right questions or get the right answers. In fact, errors and wrong guesses allow a facilitator and client to explore various avenues and gain a richer, more detailed understanding of the client's inner landscape.

Noticing bias

When someone presents a problem with which they need help, it is helpful for the facilitator to remember that the one presenting the problem is only one part of the client's personality. This narrator is frequently biased against other parts of the personality, and presents the story in a way that is already slanted to favor its own interests and goals. Like a presidential spokesperson at a press conference, the narrator paints a picture of an experience according to a biased agenda. Like a savvy journalist interviewing the spokesperson, the Process Work practitioner knows that the narrator is biased, and tries to ask questions that generate a fuller picture.

To get around the bias of the narrator, the facilitator must ask a lot of questions and obtain a full description of all the parts and their relationship. The facilitator must also recognize that the narrator tries to gain the facilitator's endorsement of its version of reality. Here again, it is useful to think of how a good journalist works. The journalist does not treat any one interviewee as the sole authority on a particular event. The event looks different to everyone who witnessed it, and by interviewing all of the witnesses the journalist is able to provide a fuller account of the event. Similarly, the facilitator is sensitive to the primary process, but does not side with its report. She includes the narrator as only one view of the whole process.

To sidestep the bias of the narrator and elicit marginalized information, asking "wicked questions" is a particularly useful technique. Wicked questions are "wicked" in the sense that they do not follow the consensus reality description favored by the primary process. They are framed outside the boundaries of the narrator's reality, and they serve to expose biases and assumed truths. For instance, a client might present jealousy as a problem, by exclaiming, "Ugh, I get so jealous when my partner is away. It's just not normal, you know!" Here the primary process, the one speaking, has a bias against jealousy, and invokes a normative view of reality to back herself up. The facilitator can stay unaligned on the issue of jealousy, and avoid taking sides for or against the narrator, by asking a question such as, "What's bad about jealousy?" This question does not collude with the speaker's assumption that jealousy is bad. Another type of wicked question investigates the relationship between inner parts, such as "What do you hate about jealousy?" When the

Exercise 3.1
Mapping a process

Work in twos: a facilitator and a client.

The client briefly describes a current problem or issue.

The facilitator follows the steps below.

1. Notice the verbal and nonverbal signals of the client to find the various parts of the process pattern, including the narrator.
   - How is "the problem" described?
     What nonverbal signals and words are used to describe it?
     What qualities belong to it?
     What words are used or emphasized?
   - Are there any other parts described?
     Do they have particular signals, words, or qualities that go along with them?
   - Can you detect a reaction to or solution to the problem?
     Can that be identified as a part?
     Does it have signals, words and qualities associated with it?

2. Using your creative imagination, make up a story or fairy tale that includes all the parts of the process. Choose one part to start with. Don't name it exactly as the client has named it. Make up a character or figure, which shares the signals and qualities of that part. It could be an animal figure, a magical figure, a character out of a movie, book or fairy tale. Start the story with "Once upon a time…."

3. As you begin to tell the story, look at the client's feedback. Notice where there is excitement and energy. Have the client fill in the critical places in the story: other characters, plot developments, and resolutions.

4. When the story telling is done, together with the client, discuss the map of the process that the story suggests. Identify the primary and secondary parts, the edges between them and their relationships to one another.

facilitator inquires about relationship between parts in this way, she begins to see how the primary process marginalizes other parts.

Exercise 3.1 offers an opportunity to practice mapping a process structure using the ways of thinking introduced so far. The exercise helps develop inductive reasoning, and the ability to gain an unbiased picture of the process structure.

Perceptual skills for mapping a process

To make a complete map of a process structure, a facilitator requires perceptual skills to distinguish amongst the multitude of verbal and nonverbal communication signals that characterize any interaction between facilitator and client. A map of process structure organizes perceptual information into two basic categories: signals that are associated with the everyday identity (primary process), and signals that are marginalized by the primary identity and carry information about the dreaming dimensions of reality (secondary process). In the next section we will describe the perceptual skills needed in mapping process structure and beginning to use it to access dreaming realities.

Sensory-grounded information

Finding patterns in perceptual information requires the use of second attention to find sensory-grounded information, the phenomenological description of dreaming experience. Sensory-grounded information appears in specific sensory and motor "channels," or modes of communication. It is found in verbal statements, both stated and implied, and in paralanguage (such as tone of voice, volume, and rhythm of speech). It is particularly evident in non-verbal signals, such as posture, gestures, movements, and facial expression. It is also found in the experience of the facilitator or other communication partner, and includes feelings, reactions and other inner experiences. Finally, the field or environment is a source of sensory-grounded information, which appears in synchronicities and other meaningful contextual events and circumstances.

Distinguishing sensory-grounded information from primary process descriptions

Asking questions and interacting with clients about their process help sensory-grounded information become more apparent to the facilitator. The facilitator's initial ideas about the process structure change and develop as more sensory-grounded information comes to hand. The facilitator forms an idea about the process based on the information available, and then asks questions to double check and elicit further information. Feedback to questions further updates the map of a process structure as it brings in more sensory-grounded information. In mapping a process, it is not enough to take what someone says at face value. In order to get the full picture, the facilitator needs to be curious and persistent, and ask about dream-like qualities of experience using questions that invite sensory-grounded description (see Box 3.1).

The following example of two friends talking about financial problems illustrates the difference between sensory-grounded information and primary process description. A woman, "Sophie," is telling her friend, "Harriet," that she is worried about money. Sophie speaks about her problems from a primary process perspective, complaining that she feels nervous, constrained, and pressured by not having enough money to pay her bills. She talks about what she thinks has caused her lack of money, what that says about her personality, what it means in terms of her future prospects, and so on.

As Sophie speaks, some of her signals are consistent with this primary process description. They relate to experiences that she identifies verbally as "me," such as "I am so worried about money these days," "I never was any good at saving," and "I think I will go ask Fred about what to do about my finances." Non-verbal signals that go along with what she is saying include her facial expression (creased forehead and tension in

---

Box 3.1

Differentiating sensory-grounded information from primary process description

Sensory-grounded signals must be identified in and of themselves, distinct from any reactions, interpretations or thoughts about them. It is often not enough to just listen to what someone says. It is helpful to interact with the person about their experience to obtain sensory-grounded information. The following questions are sometimes useful:

- How do you experience the problem?
- What is it doing to you?
- How are you aware of this problem; how do you know you have it?
- How would you give it to someone else?
- What is the essential quality or energy of this problem?
- If this problem had a personality, or was a figure, who or what would it be?

---

her lips), and other physical signals such as tense shoulders and fidgeting hands. Her primary intent (talking with her friend) is also communicated in postural and facial signals such as leaning forward and looking directly at her friend.

Simultaneously, other signals provide sensory-grounded information about Sophie's secondary process. These relate to experiences that she identifies as "not me" or as happening *to* her. In order to elicit sensory-grounded information, and explore the problem at a dreaming level, Harriet can help Sophie track experiences from which she feels split off (such as the clenching fist, gritted teeth and the "pressure maker") by asking questions such as: "How do you experience your money problem?" or "What's it like to have money troubles?" or even, "What does this worry do to your body?" In response, Sophie describes what is happening to her as a sense of pressure. She says, "I feel squeezed," and makes a hand motion, a tight clenching fist, and slightly grits her teeth. At the same time, her voice tightens. All of these are pieces of sensory-grounded information. As such, they describe the experience *itself*, rather than offering ideas about it, or expressing reactions to it.

Acquiring sensory-grounded information

Mapping a process structure involves a four-step process of acquiring sensory-grounded information: *listening* to what the client says, *looking* at what the client is doing, *sensing* the facilitator's own experiences and the field for synchronicities, and *linking* all of these steps together. In practice, these steps are not separate or sequential, but are interwoven and often simultaneous. They are discussed here separately for the sake of clarity.

Listening

A dreaming process is experienced initially as "other." It is found in statements that describe someone as "not me," such as other people, figures, events, or symptoms. These are also referred to as "third parties" or "dreamfigures." Listening for qualities, characteristics, and activities associated with third parties provides information about the dreaming process and its modes of expression. For example, if a client says, "I am having trouble with my boss," the boss is a third party, or dreamfigure. The way in which the person describes the boss provides sensory-grounded information about that dreamfigure. A client's description of her boss as "pushy and intolerant" suggests that these qualities are marginalized by her primary process.

Autonomous and unwanted experiences. Experiences that are described as troubling, disturbing, or out of the speaker's control are an indication of a secondary process. Although "I" statements often point to a primary process, they also may indicate something secondary. As a facilitator, it is useful to double check whether an "I" statement is referring to something primary or secondary, by asking oneself: "What's happening *to* the person? What does my client identify with doing, wanting, or being?" For example, someone might say, "I get tired by the end of the day." Here, tiredness is not a primary experience, but a secondary one. The speaker implies that "tired" happens to him as an autonomous experience. He does not identify with the tiredness that is happening to him; rather, he suffers from it.

Ghosts. "Ghosts" are implicit or embedded elements of the dreaming process that are found in verbal and non-verbal signals. Ghosts are implied in what is said and not said, rather than mentioned directly. Their presence is indicated by various verbal clues, found in elements of language structure, such as negations, use of tense and voice, incomplete sentences, questions, quoting, and paralinguistic clues.

Negations. Ghosts are found in negations, since to say something is *not* happening suggests that a model or concept of something exists in the mind of the speaker, but is currently being disavowed. For instance, the statement, "I feel fine. I'm not too stressed out today," indicates that stress is on the speaker's mind, but is secondary. Otherwise, the speaker might say either, "I'm fine" or "I'm stressed out."

Tense and voice. Ghosts are also found in the use of tense and voice. When a speaker uses the past tense, this suggests that something is disavowed as past, while being recollected in the present. If the speaker says, "I'm no longer stressed out," it may be true that he does not feel as badly as he did yesterday. However, he is still referencing his well being in relation to stress. Stress is still somehow in his consciousness. Use of the passive voice is similarly a helpful indication of a dreaming process. If a person says, "I'm bored these days" the ghost in that sentence is whatever is boring to the speaker, a split-off part of his process, which he feels is happening to him. There may also be a ghost of excitement or interest, which the speaker cannot access.

Incomplete statements. Ghosts are also found in "holes in language," or incomplete statements, as the following examples show. Each of the statements implies one or more questions (shown here in parentheses), such as: "I'm afraid." (Of what?) "I should be less jealous." (Of whom? Why? Who says? In contrast to what?) "I'm self-conscious." (Who's looking? Conscious of what part of self?) Ghosts can be found in answers to these questions. For example, a person might complain about feeling self-conscious. Upon further questioning, he says that he feels as though someone who dislikes his quiet, shy way of behaving is watching him. In this case, both the critical watcher, and the shyness, are ghosts.

Questions and answers. Whenever people ask questions, either directly or implicitly, both the response to the question and the respondent are ghosts. For example, a person might say, "I just don't know what to do with my life!" The implied question ("What should I do with my life?") indicates that he is deciding on different options, or visualizing different alternatives for his future. As well, he is imagining someone who does have ideas or information about his future. The alternatives he envisions, as well as the part of him that is actively seeking them and weighing alternatives, are marginalized in his original question and thus become ghosts.

Quoting. Quoting or reporting is another way of speaking that provides verbal clues about the presence of ghosts. For example, a woman who says: "My husband doesn't think therapy is useful," is reporting someone else's opinion and is also divulging her own viewpoint, albeit one marginalized by her primary process. Here, both the quoted opinion (therapy isn't useful) and the one who is quoted (my husband) are ghosts.

Paralinguistic clues. Finally, ghosts are also found via paralinguistic clues, which include tone of voice, such as sarcasm, or non-verbal sounds, such as snorts, tsks, and sighs. These often imply ghosts, such as hidden opinions, judgments, or other split-off feelings or attitudes. For example, the woman quoting her husband may sigh as she says, "My husband doesn't think therapy is useful." Her sigh might communicate a differing opinion to that of her husband, or hopelessness about his lack of interest in her.

Looking

A great deal of sensory-grounded information can be gained through observation of non-verbal signals. The body is a particularly rich source of dreaming information, expressing itself in somatic replies, gestures, movements, postures, and many other non-verbal signals. All clients communicate non-verbally. Where clients cannot communicate verbally, such as in comatose, trance, or catatonic states, information from non-verbal cues becomes particularly important.

Somatic replies. Somatic or non-verbal responses to questions are important dreaming signals, since they tend not to be associated with the primary identity of the speaker as often as verbal signals. They also tend to occur outside the speaker's awareness. For example, if a facilitator asks his client a question such as "How are you?" or "What shall we do today?" the client will always give a non-verbal response, regardless of whether or not she answers in words. If she responds verbally, her body's non-verbal answer (for example, breathing, a sigh, eye movements, stretching) will convey extra information that may or may not be consistent with her spoken response.

Physical extremities. The extremities of the body, particularly the hands, fingers, toes, and legs, are a rich site of non-verbal signals. In interaction, focus is often directed to the face (the eyes and facial expression), through which conscious intent is frequently communicated. Movement in the extremities tends to be further from awareness, and often more secondary. It is helpful to notice what the hands and feet, arms and legs are doing, and to look for those facial signals that tend to be further from ordinary awareness, such as skin coloration, swelling, watering of the eyes, quivering, blinking, and teeth, lip and throat movements.

Movement and posture. Movement signals, which include posture and absence of motion, are often a particularly valuable source of sensory-grounded information. They can be roughly divided into four categories. In one type of movement signal, postures or movements are associated with the primary intent of the client, such as looking, telling a story, or relating to another person. A second type of movement signal includes those postures and movements that accompany verbal descriptions with which the client does not identify. These signals are congruent with what the client is talking about, but belong to the "not-me," or secondary experience of the client. An example of this is a hand movement that accompanies a person's attempt to describe a vague feeling or image from a dream.

A third type of movement signal consists of postures and movements which neither have an identifiable relationship to the intent of the speaker, nor to the topic of conversation. These signals are termed "double signals." They are clear indications of a secondary process. Finally, a fourth type of movement signal consists of postures or movements that are "edge phenomena," rather than signals associated with a primary or secondary process. Such signals appear as a range of non-verbal behaviors, such as fidgeting, yawning, laughing, or expressions of physical tension. They occur at "edges" or "hot-spots," where the known identity comes into contact with the unknown.

Movement ghosts. Movements are almost always made in relation to something else, a "movement ghost." For example, if someone is stretching, it might be that she is stretching against some feelings of being constrained or tense. If someone is leaning back, what she leans against is a ghost. A wall or chair back might be a secondary experience of support or strength, an ability to hold things up. If a person curls up tightly on the floor,

---

Box 3.2
Tip for noticing non-verbal signals in movement

To practice noticing non-verbal signals in movement, ask yourself:
- What looks intended, and what looks unintended?
- Which parts of the movement do *not* go along with the story or conversation?
- Is there a movement that interrupts, or happens simultaneously with the intended movement?
- What is *almost* happening in the person's movement, but not quite yet?

---

she might be closing in to get away from something, maybe a negative figure, a sense of pressure, or something frightening.

Taking the focus off the client. The facilitator's focus can interrupt the communication of dreaming signals, since the intention to communicate, relate, or address an issue is essentially a primary process. As a facilitator, it is useful to notice what happens if you casually take your focus off the client, by looking away briefly, looking down, blowing your nose, or opening a window. Does the client look down, breathe, sigh, close her eyes, or stretch? What signals come up when the facilitator's focus is temporarily removed?

Sensing

Dreaming processes are not bound by time and space; they are field phenomena. Their signals can be found in the experience and behavior of all participants in an interaction, in the environment, in atmospheres, and in meaningful events such as synchronicities. By sensing her own experience, a facilitator has access to sensory-grounded information that is relevant to a client's process. She can access this information by noticing her own feelings, experiences, or moods, and by checking her body posture, facial expressions, and other double signals.

Box 3.3
Finding sensory-grounded information

1. Language
   - Third parties or "not-I," talking about others, states, experiences
   - Past, future or conditional tense: "I *was* sad," "I *will be* sad," "I *could be* sad."
   - Passive voice: "I am overwhelmed."
   - Missing or implied parts of sentences
   - Negations: "I am *not* sad."
   - Qualifications, hedging: "I mean..." "I think..." "I guess..."
   - Vocabulary: slang, stressed words, foreign words, forgetting a word
   - Judgments and biases: "should," "ought," "too"
2. Paralanguage
   - Speaking in other voices, accents, quoting others, sarcasm
   - Pauses, stuttering, stumbling, "uhhs," "ahh," "hmm"
   - Tone and intonation: volume, speed, rhythm of voice, pitch, stress
3. Body and posture
   - Face: eyes, lips, skin around the eyes, jaw, coloration, swelling
   - Extremities: hands, feet
   - Muscle tension: tensed, loose, slumping, rigid
   - Posture and body direction
   - Breathing, sighing, swallowing
   - Movement ghosts: leaning against something, stretching, curled away from something
4. Facilitator's experience:
   - What do you feel? What opinions, thoughts, ideas arise?
   - What flirts catch your attention?
   - What do you NOT understand fully?
       What edges in yourself do you notice?
   - What are your own double signals? What is your body doing?
   - What is happening to you?

Field phenomena. Field phenomena such as interruptions, disturbances, or strange events in a momentary interaction or in a client's account of an experience can be related to the client's process. In an example of this, Julie describes a synchronicity that happened while she was working with a client on the telephone. "Once during a session in which a client was working on a relationship conflict she had with her friend, I noticed I felt disconnected to her emotions. I checked in with myself, noticing where and when this feeling occurred. I asked myself whether my feelings related to any particular signal in my client. I realized that my client's voice had a hurt and dramatic tone to it. She was complaining that her friend was too busy, and hadn't made time to see her. I noticed that my feelings, of being disconnected, or out of tune with my client, resembled the friend. I was 'picking up' the role of the friend. At that very moment, our phone connection suddenly disconnected! When she called back a minute later, I mentioned the disconnection, the friend's disconnect and the phone company's disconnect! Immediately, my client said, 'Yes, that's what troubles me about this! She's so detached, and I'm so worked up. I feel completely desperate about this, and don't know why.' When she said that, my feeling of disconnect subsided. Now I felt we could focus on why and how she got so worked up when she felt unloved, rather than focus on the relationship conflict."

Linking

The process of linking all the information gathered from listening, looking, and sensing forms the final step in obtaining an overview of a process structure. Linking it all together involves finding clusters of signals that share an energetic quality or description. Clusters are made up of all the verbal and non-verbal signals that belong to a dreamfigure, or third party. For example, in Julie's telephone session with the client who is upset about her friend's lack of time for her, signals cluster around two main dreamfigures. A "client cluster" is found in the client's verbal signals ("upset," "hurt," and "angry") and

---

Box 3.4
Tips for Linking

- Ask yourself what signals "cluster" together, or have the same energy, quality, or quality, or description
- Identify the "not-I" (third parties and ghosts) in the client's story or conversation. Find the nonverbal signals and descriptions that belong to the dreamfigures or roles in the interaction.
- Find the nonverbal signals and descriptions that belong to the dreamfigures or roles in the interaction.
- Find the nonverbal signals and descriptions that belong to the dreamfigures or roles in the interaction.
- Identify the qualities, verbs, and channels used to describe the different roles.

---

paralinguistic signals (rising tone of voice). Another cluster, the "friend cluster," is found in verbal signals ("aloof," "detached," and "uninterested"), in atmospheric signals (Julie's experience of feeling disconnected), and in the synchronicity of the phone disconnecting.

Finding dream doors

Process structure outlines possible dream doors, or points of entry into the dreaming process. A good overview of process structure also indicates which of these dream doors is the one to enter. Rather than trying to figure out which entry point to choose, a facilitator can be guided by the sensory-grounded signals in front of her. She notices signals arising in the moment, and takes them as recommendations of how to proceed. The more she focuses on these signals, the less she has to devise where to go and what to do next.

To find a dream door, a facilitator identifies a third party or dreamfigure, its qualities, signals, and the channels in which

---

Box 3.6
Finding Dream Doors

To find a dream door, listen for third parties. For each third party, find:
- Their qualities
- Their channels
- Accompanying non-verbal and paralinguistic signals

---

these appear. If she does not have enough information to find these, she must ask questions that elicit responses in the form of more sensory-grounded information. In this way, the dream door reveals itself organically.

The following example shows how to track the flow of signals to locate dreamdoors. The facilitator and client are chatting at the beginning of a session. Notice how the facilitator uses the framework of a casual conversation to observe and track the dreaming experience.

FINDING A DREAM DOOR

CLIENT: I'm having a hard week. I just found out my car needs new brakes, and my kid wants to go on a class trip, which costs another $50, and we just don't have it. I don't know how I'm going to make ends meet.

FACILITATOR: (*Thinks that the money problem indicates several different dream doors: it could be a specific issue, like the kid, the car, or another everyday concern. It might also be the worry and anxiety, or, it might be money itself, and the sense of wealth and/or poverty. The facilitator decides to engage the topic, and see what direction the feedback indicates.*) Money worries, how difficult. Is it always this tight, or is it especially tight for you now?

CLIENT: Well, it's always been tough. You know, single mom (*pauses, looks at facilitator, smiling slightly*), no child support. It's tough. We usually do OK, but every now and then, the car, the roof, medical bills, and then...

FACILITATOR: (*Notices the client's stress on "single mom" in her intonation, and how she paused, looked at the facilitator and smiled as she said the words. She notices the client feels a sense of pride in being a single mother. She is not sure so decides to check it out.*) Hmmm, that's impressive, you're doing it all by yourself, no help, raising those kids alone, working... wow!

CLIENT: (*smiles more broadly*) Well, lots of people have to do that, but yeah, no help.

FACILITATOR: (*The smile is positive feedback to praise, so pride is definitely in there. She decides to explore more about pride and the "single mom" experience. She also notices that the client mentioned "no support," and guesses that both "help" and "no-help" are present as dream doors. Going it alone goes along with the client's pride in herself. But what about needing help, or reaching out for help? Could that be part of her process, too?*) No help! None at all? How do you manage? Do you ever wish you had help?

CLIENT: Well, actually, no. Everyone is such a deadbeat. Getting help just makes it worse, I have to rely on all these idiots. I'm better off just doing it myself.

FACILITATOR: (*"Deadbeat" is a third party, one who is not so competent. Time to ask about its qualities.*) What do you mean deadbeat? Who's a deadbeat? Why are they so useless?

CLIENT: Well, everyone's a deadbeat. I mean, even my kids. They get it from their Dad. I ask them to clean their rooms, and they just shove everything into their drawers. They break the vacuum cleaner and instead of telling me it needs to be fixed, they just put it back in the closet, and then I find it next time.

FACILITATOR: (*Wanting to find out more about the qualities of the deadbeat, she notices the client is furious at the deadbeats. She thinks she has to be careful not to collude with the client against the deadbeat, because it's a potentially useful dreamfigure. She knows her next question must negotiate the narrator's bias while gaining more sensory-grounded information.*) Wow, how do they manage to do that, seeing you work so hard all day, and then come home to a messy house?

CLIENT: Well, they're watching TV, they don't notice (*laughs*). I come home, and they're just lounging around on the sofa (*she leans back on the sofa*) like couch potatoes! (*sighs and leans back further*)

Dream door! In this example, "deadbeat" is the "third party" in the client's story, found in the children's behavior. "Deadbeat" qualities are found in words such as "lounging," "relaxing," "not noticing" and "nor caring," and in the client's nonverbal signals of leaning back, sighing, and closing her eyes slightly when she mimics the deadbeat. Clustered together, they indicate that proprioception, or body sensation, is a channel through which dreaming is being expressed, because the client describes being a deadbeat using proprioceptive language and non-verbal signals.

The client is a hard worker, and her single mom identity brings her a sense of pride and accomplishment. But she is also in conflict with other people who do not work hard and are more selfish. Being less of a workhorse for others, and more relaxed and interested in herself, may be an important new state of being for her.

Mapping the flow of process is not only a way of organizing perceptions of the client's experience, but simultaneously shows a way of entering dreaming experience through a "dream door." The more skill the facilitator has in mapping process structure, the easier it is to enter into the flow of dreaming. After entering a dream door, the next stage in following a process requires the skills of tracking signals in their various channels, and "learning the language of dreaming."

Box 3.5
Tips for finding process structure

Staying present.

If you find you are getting lost in a client's story or emotions, you are likely following only the content and not thinking in terms of dreaming signals. A helpful way to stay present is to listen to the story as a mysterious event, a dream rather than fact.

Ask for sensory-grounded information.

Ask clients to describe or reformulate what they mean. As they describe their process, look for sensory-grounded information in language, paralanguage and non-verbal signals to discover the dreaming process behind the words.

Practice on your own.

The field between client and facilitator exerts a force on the facilitator that is often felt as a pressure to respond. It can be difficult to think and perceive in a detached way while working with a client. Learn how to find process struc as a pressure to respond. It can be difficult to think and perceive in a detached way while working with a client. Learn how to find process structure by practicing *outside* the therapeutic setting in short repetitive practice sessions. Record practice sessions on video, and analyze the process structure afterwards.

Separate verbal from nonverbal signals at first.

Learn how to identify signals; separate verbal signals from nonverbal ones at first.Audiotape or write down what people say and analyze it later for process structure. Then, do the same with nonverbal signals on videotape. Without paying attention to the words, watch body signals only.

Talk to yourself.

Thinking sometimes needs company. It can be hard to know what you perceive without talking about it, reformultaiong it, and chewing it over with yourself. Talk to yourself internally as you are working, in order to make sense of what you perceive. Ask yourself:

•What disturbs my clients?

•What is the basic quality of that disturbance?

•What is marginalized or unloved here?

•What signal has been going on for the last ten minutes that I've been ignoring in order to follow the person's story?

•What feeling do I have sitting with this person, and is there a signal I am reacting to?

Find clusters of signals.

You may feel overwhelmed by hundreds of signals bombarding you. But there are not hundreds of parts, only a few. Almost all signals can be grouped into two or three clusters that share qualities or characteristics.

Chapter 4

The Language of Dreaming

Mapping a process identifies the signal clusters, or dream doors, that lead to the nonconsensus world of dreaming. After one maps a process, in order to enter the dreaming world more fully, it is important to learn how to speak its language. When visiting a foreign country, we can get around more easily, and become more deeply acquainted with the place and its people, if we learn how to communicate in the local language. The more fluent we become in speaking the language, the more the unfamiliar world opens up to us. The language of the dreaming world is a signal-based language. Becoming fluent in this language involves developing the ability to notice signals as they appear in an initial channel, and to allow them to find expression in additional channels through a process called "amplification." In this chapter, we take a detailed look at the amplification process. In particular we will explain how to use channels and feedback to amplify sensory-grounded information, and thus to establish communication with the nonconsensus world of dreaming.

Channels

Channels are signal vehicles, which convey intended and unintended communication. A channel may be "occupied" or "unoccupied." An occupied channel is one that is characterized by conscious intent. It is used to transmit a message from the primary process. An unoccupied channel carries information that is marginalized by the primary process. A channel may be irreducible or reducible, depending on whether it can be broken down into other, more basic channels. There are four irreducible channels. These are the proprioceptive channel, the visual channel, the auditory channel, and the movement channel. Each has distinct qualities or properties and may be amplified using channel-specific language.

Proprioceptive channel

In Process Work terminology, proprioception refers to felt body sensations, such as temperature, weight, and pressure. When a person describes a secondary process in the proprioceptive channel, he uses words like "hot," "cold," "heavy," "light," that convey physical sensation. Nonverbal signals, such as sighing or an altered breathing rate, may also indicate proprioceptive experience. When a person is having a physical sensation, her breathing is often deep and slow, or she may swallow. Her eyes are often cast downward, or she may close her eyes slightly longer than an average blink. Her rhythm of speech may be slower, and her posture may be slumped forward, or have a slow, downward motion. Proprioceptive experiences have a characteristic range, rhythm or intensity. For example, they can be diffuse, sharp, dull, throbbing, irregular, steady, or slow. To help a proprioceptive experience self-amplify, a facilitator can invite a client to notice the quality of the experience, by naming possible qualities such as heavy, light, diffuse, sharp, dull, throbbing, irregular, steady, or slow. She may also find it helpful to slow her own breathing, and speak in a quiet, slow voice.

Visual channel

Visual channel experiences are conveyed as images, fantasies, and pictures. The visual channel is indicated by the use of active or passive forms of verbs such as "see," "look," "notice," or "observe." Movements that indicate visual experience include upward glances, or rapid blinking. Shallower breathing is also often equated with visual experience, as is gazing away or focusing on a distant spot in space. To help a visual experience self-amplify, we might ask questions about the image's color, shape, size, texture, brightness and focus. Often, images have a context. To find out more about a visual experience, a facilitator can ask what else appears with an image, or ask the person to describe it like a scene in a movie.

Movement channel

Movement is a kinesthetic mode of experience and expression. The movement channel is evident in nonverbal signals such as jiggling feet, hand movements, shifting around in a chair, or rocking. Words that point to a secondary movement experience include action words such as "run," "fly," "move," and "go." Movement experiences have various characteristics, including speed, rhythm, direction, intensity and force. They are also characterized by space, resistance, and effort. Movements signals self-amplify most readily when the body is fully engaged. It can be useful to ask a person to stand up if a signal expresses itself in movement. Standing up allows the movement to extend naturally into more of the body.

Movement is often coupled with other channels. A coupled channel is one in which an experience is simultaneously conveyed in two channels. For instance, sometimes a movement is experienced as a body feeling. In this case, movement and proprioception are coupled. Amplifying a movement signal using the coupled channel can help it self-amplify. For example, if a client is moving with an image in mind, showing the client the movement he is making helps to amplify the movement. If a movement is coupled with proprioception, slowing it down so that it can be felt more deeply amplifies the movement.

Auditory channel

The auditory channel encompasses all manner of internal and external sounds, such as vocalization, inner dialogue, music, and noises in the environment. A person who expresses a secondary experience in the auditory channel might use phrases such as "I heard...." or "That sounds like...." Examples of secondary processes conveyed in the auditory channel include quoting others or self-reflective comments such as, "Well, that's a stupid thing I just said," or, "I know this sounds weird, but..."

Auditory signals have volume, pitch, timbre, intonation, speed, accent, and rhythm. If someone is hearing or listening to an inner or outer sound, asking about its volume, tone, or pitch helps it self-amplify. If it is a human voice, asking about the speaker and the qualities of the voice can strengthen the signal. Is it a man's or woman's voice? Is the speaker young or old? Is it a familiar voice? What language is used? Is it a dialogue or just one voice? If it is a non-human sound, does it have a rhythm? Can the person recreate the sound? Asking about the qualities of the sound amplifies it further. For example, is it a grumble or a whistle, raspy or breathy? Does it hiss, growl, howl, sing or moan?

Composite channels

As well as experiences carried in the four irreducible channels, other experiences are carried in the composite channels of the relationship channel and the world channel. Composite channels are so called because they are made up of a combination of elementary channel experiences.

Relationship channel

The relationship channel encompasses experiences or events that are communicated through, or felt in relationship to someone else. Indications of relationship channel experience are found in how people speak. For instance, if someone says, "My friend John told me that I was stubborn," this indicates that the person is experiencing a part of herself through relationship. If other people feature strongly in a person's speech, this suggests that the process is being experienced in the relationship channel.

World channel

The world channel is made up of experiences that are related to collective, global, social, or political events or institutions. People who are experiencing a process in this channel might feel that global issues or collective experiences have a powerful effect on them. They receive information about themselves through world channel experiences. Institutions or global events "happen to them." For example, a world channel experience might be an audit by the Internal Revenue Service, or being served a summons to appear in court. Accidents are coupled channel experiences, comprised of movement and world channel events. Sometimes body symptoms have world channel aspects to them. For instance, allergies are proprioceptive experiences coupled with a world channel aspect, since they involve physical reactions to substances or conditions outside the body.

Amplifying an experience using channels

The Process Work facilitator must befriend the unknown and learn to speak its language, by talking directly to dreaming signals. This involves identifying the channel in which a signal appears and unfolding it into a multi-channeled experience.

Talking directly to a dreaming signal

Each channel "speaks" a particular language, which includes a vocabulary, nonverbal expressions, and paralanguage. It is most effective to use these elements when talking directly to a signal. For instance, a body signal will self-amplify if it is addressed in the language of the proprioceptive channel, in terms of weight, temperature, or pressure. On the other hand, the self-amplification process is inhibited if a person is asked to describe an experience in a channel in the language of another channel. For instance, if someone is asked to describe a body sensation in visual terms, this shifts focus from the immediate experience of the body feeling. The primary process must translate the proprioceptive experience into a visual channel experience.

Talking directly to a dreaming signal is a way of helping a person to use their second attention to focus on unexplored experiences. The following guidelines may be helpful in developing the ability to talk directly to a dreaming experience.

Names and no-names. Names and pronouns engage a person's first attention. To speak to a dreaming signal directly, try to avoid addressing the person by name, or saying, "you." For instance, the recommendation, "Go ahead and notice what it's like to lean back" will more effectively engage the experience of leaning back than the question, "What do you notice?" This question is more likely to engage a primary, thought process about the body experience.

Commands. Using the imperative (command) form of speech helps people follow dreaming signals because it bypasses the primary process and its opinions. "Feel that" is an imperative form. Other examples of commands that amplify the dreaming experience without invoking the normal identity are "Notice what you notice," "Just feel (or see, or listen)" and "Take your time."

Blank access questions. In order to find the experience in a signal, it is helpful to use "blank access" questions that engage a nonconsensus experience directly, instead of inviting thinking, abstracting or theorizing about an experience. Questions that require a verbal answer are better avoided since they tend to invoke the primary process and its opinions.

In the following example, a client is trying to focus on the dream image of a tree. The facilitator asks, "Can you tell me what else you can see in that image?" This question engages a primary process metacommunicator. The little pronoun "me" is actually a big word. It brings attention to "me" and "you" speaking together, and the facilitator–client relationship. The pronoun "you" is separate from the image, emphasizing the fact that the person is not the image, and strengthening the edge between the primary identity and the dreaming experience. The sentence is also framed as a question that invites a verbal response. This requires the client to speak, which may be difficult when her attention is focused on a non-verbal experience. In addition, it asks her to articulate something of which she is hardly aware.

Alternatively, the therapist might ask the client, "Is the tree standing alone, or is it in a dark forest, or field, or…?" This question engages the dreaming process more directly in a number of ways. It contains no nouns or pronouns, and so does not draw awareness to the people or their relationship. All the nouns in the sentence refer directly to the dreaming experience (tree, forest, field). This focuses attention on sensory-grounded information.

Using the voice as an instrument

Talking in the language of a specific channel also involves using the voice as an instrument. It is often helpful for the facilitator to "keep the signal company" by talking to it, joining it, and dreaming into what the person is saying or doing. Using sound, especially sound that matches the channel experience, is a type of blank access. It does not add content, or bring in any kind of thought that invokes the primary process. Examples of using the

---

Exercise 4.1
Using sound to amplify experience

Two people work together
1. Person A thinks of an experience in one of three channels: the proprioceptive, channel, the visual channel or the auditory channel. The experience can be a feeling or sensation (like a pain, or pressure), an internal or external image (fantasy figure, shadow on the wall), or a sound heard internally or externally (a stomach rumbling, a refrigerator humming). Person A tells Person B what the experience is.
2. Person B helps Person A deepen the experience by asking about it, using different vocal qualities. Try altering rhythm, volume, pitch, or timbre. For instance, Person B might say, "Hmmm, go ahead and feel your knee," in a low, deep, slow tone of voice. Or, "Ahhh, a shadow. Ooohh, what shape is it?" in a breathy, light tone.

---

voice as an instrument includes encouraging comments or sounds like "mmmhmm," "yes," "great," "ahhh," "I see...."

The qualities of the various channels can all be expressed using sound. Sound waves have a deeply altering affect. For instance, many deep body sensations respond to a low frequency, achieved by speaking in low, deep, slow, resonant tones. Visual experiences sometimes have qualities of airiness or lightness. Sometimes they respond well to a light, soft, breathy, high voice with very little resonance or timbre. Experimenting with how voice quality can help amplify experiences is a useful exercise in developing the ability to unfold a process.
Both Person A and B notice the various amplifying affects of the vocal tones, and discuss together what types of sound help with the different experiences.

Guessing into an experience

Even though the goal of amplifying an experience is to stick to the "bare bones" of its sensory-grounded information, and not interpret, guessing into an experience can help people focus their second attention and deepen an experience. If a guess mirrors a channel experience, does not request a verbal response and is offered to the imagination, it can help deepen the channel experience. Whether right or wrong, guesses spark the imagination and focus the second attention. Wrong guesses will simply not be picked up, and may help a client clarify what she is actually experiencing.

Wrong guesses can make people become more conscious of what they are actually experiencing. Knowing what something is *not,* implies knowing what it is, even if a person is not immediately conscious of it. The question, "Is the tree standing alone, or is it in a dark forest, or field, or...?" offers several guesses. The client may say, "No, it's in a stand of poplars at the edge of a field," or "No, it's a big old elm on a city street." A guess may turn out to be right or wrong. Either way, it can stimulate the imaginative power of second attention, and help to generate a clearer sense of what is actually being visualized. Guessing is often more effective in eliciting sensory-grounded information than open questions such as, "What else do you see in that image?"

Reflecting

Amplifying a signal involves turning something local and immediate into something global and multidimensional. It is like water flowing from a little trickle to a stream, a river, and finally, an ocean. Reflecting is a central tool in the amplification process. As an awareness tool, reflecting is part of the development of consciousness. In infancy, being reflected makes us aware of ourselves. When a facilitator reflects the dreaming experience back to a client, she helps make conscious what has been unconscious.

Exercise 4.2
20 Questions

1. Person A chooses an experience in one channel, and tells Person B what channel it is in. Person A does not say what the experience itself is.
2. Person B asks 20 questions about the experience, using channel words and paralanguage. For instance, if Person A's experience is in the proprioceptive channel, Person B might ask, "Is it pulsing?" "Does it radiate?" "Is it hot?" "Is there a pressure?"
3. Person B gauges whether the answer is "hot," "warm," or "cold" depending on how Person A responds. Quick answers generally indicate the word is close to A's experience ("hot"). If A has to think carefully about the question, or has trouble answering, it generally indicates that the question is only "warm" or "cold."

4. Person B continues to ask questions, in order to help Person A's experience to become more sensory-grounded.

Naming what is happening in terms of body parts, movements, posture, sounds, and so on, is a useful reflecting technique. A facilitator can name body parts directly, such as muscles, limbs, hands and face, and point out what they are doing. In doing so, it helps to avoid using personal pronouns that connect the primary process to the body part, as in "your face," or "your foot." For example, a facilitator might say, "The back is arching," "That fist is clenching," "Something is slumping forward," "Eyes are closing slowly."

Speaking directly to a dreaming signal and engaging it on its own terms are also helped along by metaskills, such as enthusiasm and curiosity towards the unknown. Such metaskills excite a dreaming process, and also help a client feel accompanied at an edge to unknown experience.

Exercise 4.2 offers a way to practice speaking directly to a dreaming signal, loosely based on the guessing game, "20 questions." In this game, Person A thinks of something, and Person B must guess what it is, by asking questions that Person A can only answer with "yes" or "no." In our version of the game, Person A thinks of an experience in a particular channel, tells Person B what channel the experience is in, but does not say what the experience is. Person A can only say "yes" or "no" in response to Person's B's guesses. The object of the game is to practice the ability to talk to a signal in its own channel language, and to amplify an experience in its initial channel, until there is a channel switch or other channels are added.

The game is over when 20 questions have been asked, or when Person A's experience has deepened to the point that a channel change occurs or new channels are added. This indicates that Person B's question helped Person A get so close to her experience, that it automatically self-amplified.

Example: Person A tells Person B that she is thinking of a proprioceptive experience. Person A feels a sharp localized pressure in her knee. She doesn't say what she feels, just that it is a proprioceptive experience. After a few questions, Person B asks, "Is the sensation dull?" Person A immediately says "no." The speed of the reply suggests that Person A has a clear sense of the experience in relation to this quality. Noting this "hot" response, Person B then asks "Is it sharp?" Person A opens her eyes wide, and making a stabbing gesture with her finger, says "Yes!" The game ends here, because Person A changes channels, when she makes the stabbing gesture (movement channel). Person B can then take a turn at choosing an experience.

Feedback

Feedback signals are signals of response to an input that further reveal the nature of a process. They guide an unfolding process from its earliest stages. Feedback is like an excitement gauge. A facilitator "excites" the signals of a dreaming process by talking directly to them. The dreaming process either responds positively or negatively.

Positive feedback

Positive feedback means that dreaming signals self-amplify in response to facilitative input, and the process continues to go in the direction in which it is already headed. For example, a facilitator notices a client's tendency to slump forward, in signals such as an extra second of out-breath, or a slight drooping of the shoulders. The facilitator says, "Yes, go ahead and let yourself slump," and the client relaxes forward, letting out a deep sigh. The facilitator's suggestion is met with positive feedback, because it recommends what is already happening. The signals do more of what they are already doing. By bringing awareness to them and recommending that they continue, the facilitator helps them self-amplify. This is also illustrated in an example from Chapter 4, where the facilitator sees a small smile on her client's face as she describes herself as a "single mom." The facilitator's comment ("that's impressive, you're doing it all by yourself, no help, raising those kids alone, working... wow!") excites the dreaming signal by talking directly to it. The client's response (smiling more broadly) is positive feedback, since it is an escalation of the signal in the direction in which it was already going.

As these examples show, positive feedback is generally an energized response to an intervention. Even a negative verbal response can be positive feedback, if it is accompanied by an energetic response that indicates the excitement of a secondary process. Sometimes a verbal "no" may simply be an expression of an edge to something secondary. An everyday example of this is a host taking care of guests at a party. The host notices that a guest glances ever so slightly in the direction of the mashed potatoes. It is a tiny signal; the guest's eyes only flash once towards the potatoes, and then back to the person he is talking with. The host notices the signal and asks, "Would you like more potatoes?" The guest says, "No, thank you," with a smile and a blush, overriding his impulse to eat more potatoes. His ordinary mind, thinking about calories or saving room for dessert, says "no," but his signals (the smile and blush) suggest that some part of him does want some more potatoes. Both his "yes" and "no" responses are positive feedback to the host's question, since they signal an energetic response in an existing direction.

Negative Feedback

Negative feedback is not an absence of feedback, but an absence of excitement. A facilitator speaks to a signal, and the signal either remains the same, or its amplitude diminishes. Little energy or interest is signaled, indicating that the step the facilitator is inviting a client to take is not happening at that moment. As the above example shows, a negative verbal response to a comment or suggestion does not necessarily indicate negative feedback. Negative feedback is an important source of information for a facilitator. Even though the immediate signals are not "excited" by an intervention, this still provides the facilitator with information about the process.

Mixed feedback

Feedback may contain a mixture of positive and negative feedback signals. The facilitator's task is to figure out which part of an intervention received negative feedback, and which received a positive response. Sometimes this is not immediately clear, and the facilitator must rely on feedback to further questions to find out. In the example of the client with the slightly drooping shoulders, mixed feedback to an intervention might occur in the following way. The facilitator notes the postural signal and attempts to amplify it by saying, "Wow, you look a tired." The client straightens her drooping shoulders and looks at the facilitator quizzically. Her signals retreat and diminish rather than self-amplify.

The quickness of the client's change of posture is an energetic response, yet her signals do not self-amplify. Mixed feedback means there are various ways of understanding the response. In the above example, it is possible that the facilitator amplified the wrong signals. Or, it could be that by calling the body posture "tired," she interpreted the signals and engaged the primary process, constellating an edge. It could also be that the facilitator's tone of voice was incongruent with the inward and nonverbal nature of the signals.

If feedback is hard to read, it is possible that an intervention was not framed clearly. A confusing comment or question will elicit mixed or confusing feedback. The facilitator's comment, "Wow, you look tired," is a statement, also an implicit question ("Are you tired?") and could also possibly be heard as a judgment. The client's mixed feedback might be in response to any of these. She may wonder if she needs to answer a question or agree with the facilitator's statement. If she hears it as a statement, she may feel criticized, judged, or misunderstood. Or she may react to the facilitator's tone of voice. Clarifying an intervention may help to make feedback clearer and easier to read.

Metaskills for working with feedback

Two of the most helpful metaskills for working with feedback are curiosity and a non-judgmental attitude. Facilitators sometimes misconstrue negative feedback as "wrong," or as an indication of poor facilitation. However, both negative feedback and positive feedback indicate a direction in which to proceed. If a therapist's question is met with negative feedback, this does not mean the facilitator is "wrong" for asking the question. By maintaining an attitude of curiosity about the unknown and a lack of concern about right or wrong moves, a facilitator uses negative feedback as a valuable way of gaining a clearer understanding of the nature and structure of a process. Like a chemist who forms an hypothesis about the kind of liquid she has in her test tube, and tests the hypothesis by heating, cooling, or adding other liquids to it, a facilitator makes interventions and notices their outcome, without judging them as good or bad. The chemist adds a little water to her mystery liquid and sees that nothing happens. She thinks, "Aha, it can't be oil in there, because oil and water would separate." She does not think, "Well, that was a stupid thing to do, because nothing happened." Similarly, the facilitator makes use of the information provided by negative and positive feedback without judgment or self- criticism.

Using feedback in following a process

Feedback is not only a specific, momentary response to an intervention; it is also an ever-present compass, pointing in the direction of the dreaming process. Following the subtle signals of a dreaming process is like crossing a river on stepping-stones.[35] Looking at the far bank doesn't help cross the river. But focusing on the stone immediately ahead is a way to get to reach the far bank. Following feedback is like using stepping-stones to cross the river. Each step forward is determined by the feedback, and signal-by-signal, the feedback leads deeper into the unknown experience.

Feedback as a somatic reply

As communication theorist Watzlawick said, "We cannot not communicate."[36] We are constantly dreaming, and therefore constantly communicate secondary process signals. Consequently, whenever we communicate with someone, we send two sets of replies: the more conscious (usually verbal) response, and the lesser known secondary signals, which are frequently somatic. Attention to unintended somatic signals (double signals) can be used at any time to gather information, and to identify the next step in amplifying and unfolding a process.

If a facilitator asks, "What shall we do next?" the double signals of the client will suggest a way, even if he says, "I don't

---

[35] Thanks to Kasha Kavanaugh for helping develop this metaphor.

[36] Paul Watzlawick, et al. *The Pragmatics of Human Communication*, 48.

Exercise 4.3
Following Feedback

This exercise provides practice in following feedback signals.
Two people sit together, as facilitator and client.

1. The facilitator asks three blank access questions:
   • What shall we work on?
   • How shall we work on it?
   • Where shall we go next?
2. The facilitator tries to use dual awareness: first and second attention.
   • Use first attention to notice the verbal answer
   • Use second attention to notice somatic feedback (body responses).
3. The facilitator follows the nonverbal feedback.
   • Help somatic signals self-amplify by encouraging the client to go further in their direction. (e.g. "I notice you lean slightly forward," or, "Hmm, your eyes closed a bit. Maybe they want to do that more?").
   • Do not ask about the signals, since this engages the primary process.
4. Swap roles and repeat.

---

know." His somatic reply is a form of feedback, which points in the direction of his dreaming process. If he drops his head, closes his eyes and is quiet before answering, this suggests that a direction lies in going inside, feeling or meditating. If he stretches and moves around, this indicates that movement is happening, and that something wants to express itself through movement. The body always provides an answer, and indicates where to go next.

Feedback as consensus

Feedback is a way of gaining consensus among the various parts of the person, and between the facilitator and client, about how to proceed. Gaining consensus is a complex process that involves reading different sets of signals from various parts of the personality. A facilitator may not know which set to follow or may sense that one part of the personality will be offended if it is overridden by another part. Working with feedback involves facilitating the relationship between sets of signals, rather than following any one particular set.

If a facilitator detects hesitation, she must inquire about it. For example, a client hesitates while talking about a painful experience in her life. The facilitator asks, "Shall we keep going in this direction? Since you brought it up, you probably want to talk about it. Yet, you are also hesitating. Perhaps it's not the right moment, or I am not the right person for you to do that with?" By respecting the hesitation, and naming some possible positions that are implicit in the client's signals, the facilitator supports the part of the client that wants to talk and the part that does not. This helps the client come to an inner consensus about how to proceed.

Consensus and ethics

Obtaining consensus about how to proceed is an ethical consideration. It is not necessarily right to explore a signal, just because it becomes "excited" by an intervention. Consensus means that the various parts of the client's process agree on a particular direction. It requires that the intervention be framed clearly. This is especially important in situations where clients have been punished for trying to uphold their boundaries. In a situation where there is a power differential, nonverbal signals are especially important. The client might not feel free to state her opinion directly. Or she may consent to a facilitator's suggestion or line of questioning, in order to please the facilitator, out of a general submissiveness to authority, or out of fear of conflict. Through careful attention to subtle and overt signals, a facilitator can support a client's ability to set boundaries and control the interaction.

Relationship to the presenting problem

Feedback signals also communicate a client's relationship to a presenting problem and to the therapeutic process in general. Some clients come to address a specific problem, while others are not interested in problem solving. Some need to get something off their chests, or are seeking support. Others come for education, information, or to learn how to follow their inner experiences by themselves. Still others need to learn how to conflict with an authority figure. The ability to use feedback to understand a client's underlying motivations may help a facilitator not to view a client erroneously as "resistant," or become frustrated by the work in some way.

Signals show a client's relationship to the process. For example, signals such as sighing, looking down, or using a cynical tone of voice may indicate that a mood of hopelessness needs to be addressed before working on the presenting problem. A client who tells stories, or fragments of stories, without naming a central issue may need help focusing, or might need support to move off the topic altogether. Directive signals, such as not answering questions, changing direction, interrupting, disagreeing, or constantly correcting the facilitator, may indicate an "inner facilitator" who is trying to follow herself. Comments and self-talk which imply standards and judgment, including words like "should," "better," "supposed to," "bad," and "good," might suggest that the client's relationship to a process is dominated by a critical part. Questions and statements related to thinking, reasoning, and finding explanations might mean a rational approach to exploring a process is needed. Finally, if a client switches from one part to another, without comment or in a disjointed fashion, methods for unfolding a process without meta-communication may be required.

In the following example, Julie describes her work with a client, "Jeremy", on a painful story of abuse. This example shows how the client's feedback suggested a method for working on the process. "Jeremy told me about his mother's suicide and his subsequent abandonment by his father, who was alcoholic and

---

Box 4.1
Signals that suggest how to work on a process

Fragmented or disjointed story telling, without stated focus suggests a need for framing or moving off the topic.

Mood signals (e.g. not answering questions, looking down, a cynical tone of voice) invite initial work on a feeling state.

Directive signals (e.g. not answering questions, interrupting, disagreeing) may indicate an "inner facilitator" trying to follow herself.

Evaluative orjudgmental comments and self-talk (use of words like "should," "better," "supposed to," "bad," "good") suggest a critical part might need to be brought into awareness.

Questions and statementsimplying a need to think, reason, and find explanations, suggest that rational thought is a implying a need to think, reason, and find explanations, suggest that rational thought is a way to explore the process.

Flipping radically from one experience to another, without com ment or segue, invites methods for unfolding without the use of meta-communication.

---

violent. When Jeremy tried to contact his father later in his life, the father refused to have anything to do with him. It was a terribly painful story, and I could see that Jeremy was on the verge of tears as he told it. I was in pain listening to it. I commented on the amount of suffering Jeremy must feel, but he didn't respond to me. Even though his lip was trembling, his eyes watering, and his voice wavering, he ignored my focus on his feelings.

Suddenly Jeremy made an odd, joking comment. He said his childhood was so bad it could have been a movie. As he made that comment, he looked out into the room, as if he were watching a movie. His eyes fixed on a space in the room, and I noticed signals of excitement and energy as he talked about his personal story as if it was a drama of love, tragedy, abuse, and survival. This narrative style was evident in a set of signals, which indicated Jeremy's relationship to his process. Jeremy was attempting to work on the experience from a detached perspective. Noticing these signals and following their recommendation, I had an idea about how to work with Jeremy on his painful childhood experiences. I said, 'Yup, it does sound like a movie. I can even see the different actors. Who would play your father, for instance?' Jeremy's eyes lit up! He quickly named a famous Hollywood actor, known for playing tough, wise-guy roles. We then began to co-create a movie about the family drama. I encouraged Jeremy to play whatever role he chose, including the role of director, and to create a new ending to the story. By following signals that indicated Jeremy's relationship to his process, we found Jeremy's own organic way of addressing his pain."

The language of dreaming brings us closer to people's experiences and more able to follow them in an intimate way. We not only tune into the details of these experiences, but also align ourselves with each person's unique way of unfolding them. As we go further into the unfolding process, dream figures and altered states of consciousness emerge. In the next chapter we will explore methods for going deeper into the world of non-ordinary experience.

Chapter 5

Inhabiting the Dreaming World

So far, we have looked at initial stages of unfolding, which involve mapping a process structure, identifying "dream doors," and communicating with dreaming signals through feedback and channel awareness. In the later stages of unfolding, the Process Worker becomes more and more immersed in the dreaming world, by relating to the dreamfigures that populate it, and becoming familiar with their ways of being. These figures emerge through the amplification of signals in one channel into a multi-channeled experience. The world of non-ordinary experience, which feels alien and inaccessible to the everyday mind, begins to feel familiar and comfortable. In this chapter we will explore concepts, skills and attitudes that help us inhabit this world more fully. These include globalizing, shapeshifting and role-playing.

Globalizing

Globalizing means unfolding dreaming signals beyond the channel in which they initially appear. It involves building out an experience by adding more channels, or changing from one channel to another. Signals have a natural tendency to self-amplify when they are addressed in their own language. Globalizing is the next step in this self-amplification process, where signals change from local experiences (small signals in a specific channel) into diversified (multi-channeled) ones. For instance, a person who is working on an experience of cramping might first focus on the sensation of the cramp. As he feels the cramp, noting its tense, twisting quality, he spontaneously begins to make small movements with his facial muscles and with a fist, expressing the cramp energy. He then clenches and twists both fists, and more of the muscles in his body, until his whole body is involved in the experience.

Adding and switching channels

Adding or switching channels is a way of expanding an experience. Usually, it is not necessary to think about or guess which channel to add, because this emerges spontaneously through the amplification process. By paying close attention to muscle tension, body extremities, facial coloration, breathing, and posture, a facilitator can see when a new channel is emerging, and when there is a channel switch. The following example illustrates this. A woman is fascinated by a dream image of a tree. In working on her dream, she recalls the image of the tree. As she focuses on it, seeing the details of the tree and its surroundings, her posture spontaneously changes subtly. She sits up straighter, and becomes very still. In this way her experience of the tree in the visual channel expands into two more channels: movement and proprioception. Spontaneously, she adopts a tree-like posture and feels into it as a proprioceptive experience. Through these additional channels, she experiences the tree more fully. She understands it experientially, by feeling it in her body, and adopting its stillness. The multi-channeled experience of sitting like a tree, sensing the tree in her own body, and seeing the world from the tree's perspective, allows her access to "tree-like" aspects of herself.

Switching channels at an edge

Sometimes channels switch spontaneously without deepening an experience. This is called "switching channels at an edge." Switching channels at an edge leaves behind the information contained by the channel, because it brings a person back to a primary process. Second attention shifts to first attention, with a corresponding change in energy and focus.

The example of the woman working on a dream image of a tree can also be used to illustrate switching channels at an edge. The woman sees the image of the tree, which she describes as "firm" and "rooted." As she describes this image, she sits very still with her eyes closed. Suddenly she opens her eyes and says, "Now the tree is swaying in the breeze." She gets up and begins to sway vigorously. Several things suggest that these are signals of coming to an edge. First, there is an incongruity between the woman's initial stillness and her sudden swaying movement. This incongruity and the abruptness of the change suggest that an edge to stillness might be involved. Second, the woman is able to sway without hesitation. This suggests that the movement is closer to her existing ideas and experiences, rather than a deepening of a dreaming experience.

Coupling channels to access secondary information

Dreaming signals tend to appear in unoccupied channels. People may find it difficult to amplify experience in an unoccupied channel because they have no existing pattern, language or concept for what is experienced there. They just draw a blank. Here, coupled channels are often helpful. Coupled channels use a more known channel to access information in a less known channel. Coupling channels is like using a bucket to draw water from a deep well. A coupled channel serves as a medium of communication between everyday awareness and unknown experience. For instance, a person who is uncomfortable with proprioceptive experience might make a mental image (visual channel) of a body feeling, instead of trying to feel it directly (proprioceptive channel).

The following example illustrates the use of coupled channels. A man is working with a facilitator on a symptom of muscular weakness. The man is shy about his body. He does not feel comfortable moving or working directly with body sensation. The facilitator asks him what his muscle weakness feels like. He says he does not know. Taking this as a sign of an edge to experience in an unoccupied channel, the facilitator then asks what a weak muscle would look like, and suggests that the man make a picture of one. The client looks up, thinks for a moment, and replies, "Like the rubber toy, Gumby."[37] Using the visual channel as a "bucket" to dip into the movement channel, the facilitator then asks, "Can you see Gumby? What is he doing?" The client thinks for a moment, and says, "He's walking around, sort of bobbing and weaving, like he's drunk." As he says the word "drunk," he sways his shoulders and rolls his head a bit, mimicking Gumby's walk while still sitting in his chair. The channels are now coupled. The visual image helps the man slip into movement. This is easier for him, because the more easily accessible image of "Gumby" gives him a pattern for exploring unknown experiences in movement.

Working with dreamfigures

A dreamfigure is a personification of dreaming tendencies, which coalesce momentarily into a role or character. It is fluid, transitory and capable of transformation. The term "dreamfigure" is often used interchangeably with "role," "part," and "ghost." As a process unfolds, dreaming signals may develop

---

[37] Gumby is the name of a toy figure made from rubber. His limbs twist around easily, allowing him to be twisted into different shapes.

into a dreamfigure, or into an interaction between two or more dreamfigures. In either case, the focus of the work shifts to the world of the dreamfigure, its story, mindset, and way of relating to others. This stage of unfolding leads the facilitator and client "off the map," into a dreaming reality that leaves behind the ideas and interpretations of the everyday mind.

Finding a dreamfigure's mindset

Two kinds of thinking may be employed in making sense of a dreamfigure and finding its mindset: waking logic and dreamland logic. Waking logic uses interpretation, association, and memory. For example, waking logic might interpret the dreamfigure of a tree as a symbol of growth, life or stability, or associate the tree with one that figured strongly in childhood. Dreamland logic brings experiential meaning to a dreamfigure, outside the norms of consensus reality. Meaning emerges from "shapeshifting" or imagining oneself as the dreamfigure. By stepping into the experience of a tree, the woman whose work is described earlier in this chapter is able to experience the mindset of "tree-ness."

This type of shapeshifting happens spontaneously, as signals express themselves in multiple channels and are noticed by a facilitative awareness. A person feels, sees, speaks, and moves in the manner of a dreamfigure, and then explores the mindset of the dreamfigure in order to understand its meaning or message. This can be illustrated by going further with the example of the man working on muscular weakness. The man amplifies the "Gumby" experience until he feels a rubbery, flexible experience in his own muscles. He overcomes his reluctance to move by sitting like "Gumby." He lets his limbs flop, his head roll around, and his torso sway. He becomes loose, relaxed and floppy. Then he explores the mindset of the "Gumby" dreamfigure, by feeling into its floppiness as a loose, relaxed attitude. The facilitator helps him by asking, "What kind of attitude or state of mind goes with this way of sitting and flopping around?"

Exercise 5.1
Unfolding through shapeshifting

Two people work together.

Person A, as facilitator, leads Person B through the following steps:

1. Briefly describe a current issue that interests or troubles you. Then put it aside until the end of the exercise, and shift your focus to your body experiences.
2. Think of a symptom or body experience that interests or troubles you. Describe the symptom in sensory-grounded terms. What sensations do you experience? What does *it* do? What is *its* energy like?
3. Determine which channel Person B uses to describe the symptom. What words and non- verbal signals describe it?
4. Increase the amplitude of the signal in that channel. Ask about the qualities of the experience in that channel, using the language and voice tone associated with it (e.g. "Is it sharp or dull?" "Is the pressure steady, or does it fade in and out"?)
5. Notice the self--amplifying tendencies of the channel. If it is a movement, is there a sound? If a picture, does it have movement? Add more channels.
6. Add the mind-set, thought and feeling world of this experience.
7. What kind of figure is it?
8. How does the figure help with or address the issue from step one?

Swap roles and repeat.

Here is an example of unfolding using multiple channels and shapeshifting to find the mindset of a dreamfigure, and how that can be used to solve everyday problems. A client, John, tells the facilitator, April, that he is upset with his relatives who, in his view, are too interfering and nosy about the birth of the baby that he and his wife are expecting. They then put this aside, and John describes a body symptom that has been troubling him lately, stiffness in his knees. April encourages John to describe the symptom in detail. John says he feels stiff and tight when he wakes up. As he says this, he hunches over a bit, pulling his shoulders together, and folding inward. April notices the words, and movements, and also that John's muscles contract as he hunches. She amplifies this by saying what she sees, "Yes, you look like you're pulling your shoulders in really tightly." As she says this, John increases his movements slightly, and now his fingers curl slightly into a fist. Noticing that John's movement begins to globalize, or move to other parts of his body, April encourages this by saying, "Yes, go ahead and pull all the way in."

Motivated by the positive feedback she receives, April asks John to notice his posture, and imagine a figure or character that comes to mind. After a few minutes, John says that the posture reminds him of a grumpy old troll. As he says this, he smiles ever so slightly. April asks him what about that makes him smile, and he says it's fun to imagine the troll, because it doesn't care about being polite or nice to people. As John spontaneously amplifies the mind-set of the troll, April encourages him to imagine becoming the troll, by moving, feeling, thinking, or acting troll-like. Amused by what he imagines, John laughs, and says he imagines a stiff old troll, hobbling and grumbling around the room, whacking people and things with his big knobby cane. April and John have a good laugh at this image, and April asks how the troll might be helpful with John's problem with his relatives. John laughs, "Somehow, I just don't see this grumpy old troll being bothered by relatives!" "Why not?" asks April. John thinks for a moment, and says, "Being a troll is like being an old soul. I'm bothered by my relatives because I'm all caught up in their expectations and needs, but the troll is beyond all that. He just follows his own path, under the bridge, unperturbed by the comings and goings of the pedestrians above him."

Roles and role-playing

So far we have explored methods for amplifying signals using within-channel amplification, adding and switching channels, coupled channels, shapeshifting, and exploring the world and mindset of a dreamfigure. Next we will outline ways of exploring these new experiences, with particular focus on role-playing.

Role-playing in historical context

Role-playing is an ancient technique that originally used dramatic enactment to resolve conflict in a ritualistic fashion, as a form of community catharsis, and as a way of participating in creation myths and non-ordinary realities. Jacob Moreno, the founder of Psychodrama, was a pioneer in the use of role-playing techniques in western psychotherapy. His student, Fritz Perls, extended these techniques in developing Gestalt psychotherapy. Role-playing is now a common psychotherapeutic technique, recognized in many psychotherapeutic modalities as a valuable way of working with inner and outer conflict. It is involves acting out different parts and figures to gain a deeper understanding of an experience. Role-playing is also used outside individual psychotherapy, in a range of problem-solving, training and skill-building settings, in group work, mediation, conflict resolution, and performance work.

Role- playing as deep democracy

Role-playing is often used as a method of negotiation and conflict resolution between it enacts opposing positions. In Process Work, role-playing is also used in this way, but its main purpose is as a means of amplification. As in group work, role-playing in individual and relationship work is based on the principle of deep democracy. It uses interaction between roles to unfold the double signals that emerge through the interaction, and to bring marginalized experiences to light. Parts that are disliked or unknown are recognized and encouraged to interact. The interaction then becomes a vehicle for the conscious integration of previously marginalized parts.

Role-playing as shapeshifting

In processing polarization between parts, role-playing often involves shapeshifting, or entering into the multi-channeled experience of a role and taking on its worldview. This is illustrated in the dialogue below between a facilitator "Rita" and a client "Vicky". The dialogue shows how role-playing and shapeshifting can be used to unfold the different roles or parts of a dreaming process.

USING ROLE-PLAYING IN UNFOLDING

RITA: *(A facilitator)* Hello Vicky, how are you doing today?

VICKY: *(The client, a freelance technical writer, working on a users' manual for a computer company.)* Well, I've been having a hard time on my project. It's hard going, and I feel that the company is getting impatient. Even though in the contract, it's not really due until spring, I think they want to push ahead production and roll out this latest software earlier than planned. I had a talk with the guy yesterday, and he asked if it was possible to see a draft at the end of next week. It's nowhere near draft stage.

Anyway, I had a dream last night that I think relates to this problem. I was at work, but it was in Alaska. The whole department was meeting to determine who would handle an account. It was a very prestigious account. This manager, a really conservative woman, was organizing the discussion. She had us all sit in concentric circles, the highest-ranking people on the inside, and the lower ranking people on the outside. I was afraid that my contribution would be overlooked. And John was there. He told the woman to put me in the inner circle. *(Looks very serious and worried.)*

RITA: You look worried. Does something worry you?

VICKY: Well, yes. As I tell it, I realize I don't feel appreciated. It seems the men get the recognition just because
they're men, not because of their skill or contribution.

RITA: Who do you mean?

VICKY: Well, in the dream, the manager said Tom should be
in there, but Tom has nothing to do with that project,
whereas I've been central to it for years. It feels like
someone is ranking people, but according to really
superficial standards. *This last sentence uses passive construc-
tion: "It feels like someone is ranking people...." It indicates a
ghost role, the one who ranks people.*

RITA: Who is the ranker?

VICKY: Well, in the dream it was the manager. She wanted
everything ordered, really conservative. *She makes a hand
movement, like a karate chop, indicating a straight line.*

RITA: Oh! Show me again, how do you do that? *Through her
question, she speaks directly to the signal of the dreamfigure, the
chopping movement associated with the manager in the dream.*

VICKY: Like this. *She makes the chopping movement, but this
time, other signals go along with it. She sits up. Her posture
straightens, and her face gets a severe look. The dream figure of
the woman is organically emerging.*

RITA: I see. Hello. *She speaks directly to the figure.* What do
you think about it?

VICKY: *(Playing the woman)* This is right, this is the way to do
it! *She makes the hand motion again.* If it's not perfect like
this, it's bad.

VICKY: *(Now out of the role)* It's funny, being that woman for
some reason makes me think of Alaska!

RITA: Why, what about Alaska?

VICKY: Well, in a way, it's like the opposite. Alaska's so,
so...wild and loose. *She relaxes her posture, slumps a bit and
makes a waving gesture with her hand.* People say it's the last
frontier, lawless, and rugged. Its just, like, well nature.
No laws, no...tight little circles or ranking of people
according to arbitrary characteristics. It's the wilderness,

and it doesn't care about people's social standing. If you survive, that's rank! *Seeing her signals talking about Alaska the facilitator thinks she might unfold them to find the dream figure of "Alaska." But out of curiosity, she decides to find the dreamfigure through association.*

RITA: If Alaska could be represented by a figure, who might represent that quality?

VICKY: Well, actually John, the guy in the dream who included me. He's kind of a slob, somewhat rough. He reminds me of Alaska.

RITA: Could you be him, show me how he relates?

VICKY: *(Slumps back, and sticks her legs out. Her eyes close for about a half-minute. She then opens her eyes and speaks in the role of John)* Hmmm, well, people don't matter. What people think, how they view other people is irrelevant. All this stuff…it's meaningless.

RITA: *(Improvising, and picking up role of the manager in the dream.)* Well, things have to be done. Projects completed. Some people are better for the job than others.

VICKY: *(Still in the role of John. Takes a deep breath.)* Yeah, well, only in this world. Only 9-5 city life. *In the role of John, she starts to look dreamy. Her eyes close again.*

RITA: *(Still playing the woman in the dream.)* Well, what do you mean, in this world? There only is one world, right? The world of work, and you're just being lazy and unprofessional!

The client, in the role of John, doesn't respond verbally to this statement, but smiles and leans back even farther.

RITA: *(Coming out of role.)* I notice you smile, your eyes are closed, and you're leaning back. Go more fully into the body feeling of that role. Forget about the dialogue for a moment and just go far into that state. Notice what's in there.

VICKY: *(Leans back, and closes her eyes. She breathes slowly and deeply, and is quiet for a good long minute. Then she opens her eyes.)* You know, this role is so interesting. It's ruthless, yet incredibly nurturing. It's like nature, I guess. Ruthless in the sense that it doesn't care one bit about all that stuff, about work, projects, people and their worries. Yet nurturing, because it's so deep, warm, and calm inside. It's like being a rock. Nothing moves or worries it. It's so… ancient, or eternal.

RITA: Mmm, that's nature in you. What a deep state.

VICKY: Yeah, if I think about the project, or that woman, I just don't care. I mean, I care. But from this state of mind, it's so….inconsequential. I mean, I do my best, and they'll have to pay me either way. Their scheduling issue isn't my problem. *Vicky is now coming out of the role a bit.* I realize that I push myself so much, constantly seeing myself in comparative terms to other consultants, especially to my male colleagues. It's like I *am* that manager, evaluating myself, and pushing myself to do well, to do better than others, to be more professional. It's funny that you said "unprofessional!" I always fear that I'm not professional enough.

RITA: How so?

VICKY: Well, I always fear that I'm too casual. *(Laughs)* I mean, in a way, I already do feel like John, kind of slobby and down-home. When I have to go to the company meetings, it's such an effort to get dressed up. I really just want to shuffle in, wearing my bunny slippers and plaid pajamas *She laughs again.* I guess I'm already like Alaska, just rough 'n' ready!

Finding the roles in double signals

Roles are found in a person's double signals, in their symptoms and body experience, in dreams, in projections and in relationship stories. Sometimes role-plays may feel superficial, because they have not yet arrived at the essential nature of the role. This happens if we try to get to the role through the primary process, through ideas and interpretations, rather than through sig-

---

Box 5.1
How to deepen a role-play

- IF: Talking about the role, not speaking from within it.
  THEN: Become the role, speak from it in the first person.
- IF: The role is talking about other roles.
  THEN: Switch into the role that is being spoken about.
- IF: Acting out a role, role-play is superficial.
  THEN: Pick up double signals, use unoccupied channels.

---

nals and association. In the example above, the facilitator, Rita, "found" the role of the manager in the client's signals as she described the woman. Vicky made a slight hand movement, and sat up straighter, as if her body was taking on the role. This was an organic development of the role, which the facilitator noticed and encouraged further. Vicky went from the movement to the role rather easily, because it was already happening in her signals. Finding roles in double signals is especially helpful when a role-play seems stuck, lacks energy, or is somehow not working.

Various kinds of double signals may indicate that a role-play has not yet gone far enough. A client may talk about a role, but not speak from within it. Here the role-play appears not to have gone deep enough because the client still identifies as herself, thinking about the role. In order to occupy a role fully, a client must be able to talk in the first person, as the role itself. Another indication of a need to deepen a role-play is suggested when a client adopts one role, and then talks about another role. The role that is being spoken about is secondary. By switching into the role that is being discussed, the client is more likely to find the dreaming experience that is happening organically. This is illustrated in the dialogue between Rita and Vicky. Playing the role of the manager in her dream, Vicky talks about "John." The role of "John" is a disavowed part of the manager role. When Vicky switches into the role of "John", the role-play goes deeper. Finally, an indication that a role-play is too superficial is found when a client looks like her normal self while acting out a role. The role-play stays close to the client's primary process ideas about the role. In order to go into the role more fully, a facilitator can help the client to notice double signals, enter unoccupied channel experiences, and access something outside the client's normal identity.

Content versus process

In some instances, the signals of one figure in a role-play are more helpful in accessing dreaming experiences than the dialogue between the roles. This is seen in the example of Rita and Vicky, when the facilitator, in the role of the manager, challenges "John's" statement about "this world" and he responds non-verbally. The facilitator's focus shifts from the dialogue between the roles, to the double signals in "John's" posture and facial expression: his leaning back, smile and closed eyes. Through the process of unfolding the double signals of the role of "John," the dreaming experience implicit in it is unfolded more deeply.

Unfolding role-play dialogue

Focusing on double signals in verbal dialogue between roles is also useful in unfolding a dreaming process. When the role of "John" speaks dreamily of "this world," a dream door is indicated. "This world" implies the ghost of "another world." If facilitator and client were not engaged in a role-play at this point, Rita might ask Vicky about this directly by saying, "What do you mean when you say 'this world?' Are there other worlds?" Since the verbal signal "this world" comes up in a role-play, Rita unfolds it through the role-play dialogue. In the role of manager, she says disparagingly, "Well, what do you mean, in this world? There only is one world, right? The world of work, and you're just being lazy and unprofessional!" She unfolds the dream door of "another world" by provoking Vicky in the role of "John."

When a facilitator takes on a role, her job is to unfold the signals of the client's role through the character of the role she is playing. To do this, she employs double signals as a means of unfolding, as we have just illustrated. This deliberate use of double signals involves doing two things at once: acting as antagonist or protagonist, and unfolding the signals in the client's role. For instance, in the role of the manager, the facilitator says disparagingly to the role of "John," "What do you mean, 'this world,' there is only one world, isn't there?" The facilitator's question here contains two signals. One is found in her challenging tone of voice, with its implied disagreement or criticism. The other is an implied request for more information, which invites the client to go more deeply into what she has said. It is important to note that if the disparaging signal is too strong, it may interrupt the unfolding process. If, in the role of the manager, Rita had said scornfully, "What a stupid thing to say, 'this world,'" and did not ask for any more information, the dreaming about another world might not have unfolded, or the dialogue might have shut down altogether.

Following non-verbal replies

As already noted, all verbal questions are met with non-verbal replies. In a role-play, non-verbal responses are full of clues and information about the deeper or less familiar aspects of a role. Sometimes the non-verbal signals that accompany a role in a role-play are particularly helpful in unfolding a process. By looking for non-verbal signals as a client plays a role, the facilitator can find the next step in the interaction. For instance, in the role-play between "John" and the manager, "John's" non-verbal replies contain much more information than his speech. Rita helps to unfold these non-verbal signals both from within the role of a dreamfigure, as well as from her role as facilitator.

Sometimes the dialogue in a role-play comes to a standstill, or starts to repeat itself. The next step in the interaction is found in non-verbal replies. In some cases, dialogue stops because the figure that the facilitator is playing does not know how to respond. If this happens, there is no longer a pattern for the secondary role, and the facilitator is uncertain if her response will unfold the process, or take it in another direction. At this point, the facilitator can suggest that the client take over the role. She can also guess into the next step while paying careful attention to the client's non-verbal reply. In either event, the facilitator need not resolve the impasse because the way forward will be suggested by the roles themselves, through their non-verbal signals.

In some cases, a client is unwilling to play a role because it is too secondary, or she is unsure how to play it. In this situation, the facilitator can play the disliked role, and the client can interact with it. At some point in the interaction, a role switch may emerge organically. The client becomes interested in the secondary role, played by the facilitator, and is willing to play it. Alternatively, if the client does not want to switch roles with the facilitator and play the secondary role, the facilitator can pick up the client's non-verbal signals as she plays the more primary role. This is a less confrontational approach than pushing a client to play the difficult role. It works because theoretically, the secondary role is found in the double signals of a primary role. Following those signals will lead to the essential energy of the secondary role, without the client having to confront the edge directly. This is easier for the client because it involves playing a role closer to her everyday identity.

This is illustrated in the example below, in which Quincy, a facilitator, is working with Angela, a client. They are working on Angela's dream in which a severe and imposing authoritarian figure appears as a judgmental teacher, who berates Angela for being late to class. To begin with, Quincy takes the role of the judge, because Angela says she does not want to take it. She says that she hates that figure. The role-play begins as Angela speaks out against the judge and Quincy plays the teacher.

PLAYING A SECONDARY ROLE

QUINCY: *(as the teacher)* You are late. There's no excuse.

ANGELA: Back off. I'm just human, be a little understanding. *Stands with her hands on her hips, and her chin jutting forward, defiantly.*

QUINCY: *(as the teacher)* There is nothing to understand. You are late, and that's that. Any excuse is just not taking responsibility for your actions.

ANGELA: Oh give me a break. You're so uptight. So what if I'm late! I'm here now, aren't I? *Her voice is rising, and growing increasingly tense.*

QUINCY: *(as the teacher)* Well, you're just irresponsible. *He starts to feel he's at the end of the pattern, because when Angela says, "You're uptight," the "teacher" doesn't know what to say. Quincy suggests to Angela that they switch roles, and Angela play the teacher. But Angela doesn't want to switch, because she hates the authoritarian teacher. Quincy therefore decides to focus on Angela's body signals in the role that Angela is playing. He notices that Angela's forcefulness has the power and energy of the authoritarian figure, yet Angela identifies as the "weak" student.*

QUINCY: *(out of role)* Notice what your body is doing as you speak back to me as the teacher. Notice your movements and posture.

ANGELA: *Stands still for a moment, with her eyes closed.* I notice I'm leaning forward, kind of aggressively, and my hands are on my hips.

QUINCY: Go ahead, and do it even more. Feel into that. What's it like if you do it even more?

ANGELA: Well, I feel powerful and confident. Like this guy can't say anything to me! *Smiles and swaggers defiantly.*

QUINCY: I like your smile! It looks kind of like, "You can't touch me!"

ANGELA: *Smiling more.* Yeah, I'm the boss, not him!

In this example, the more secondary role is contained in the double signals of the "victim" of the teacher, the student role, with whom Angela identifies. Angela does not want to pick up the teacher figure, because her association to the figure is too negative. But her double signals display the confidence, authority and power of the role she dislikes. This is a non-verbal approach to picking up the essential quality or energy of a role. If Quincy had focused only on the negotiation or content-level of the role-play, he might have gotten stuck and missed Angela's confidence and authority. Angela might have remained too close to her normal identity of feeling powerless and pushed around by outer authorities.

Role-play theatre

Dreaming experience is often dramatic, and unfolding often takes cooperation, creativity and imagination on the part of the facilitator and client alike. When dreaming figures emerge, a story tends to unfold. A useful role-playing technique is entering into the story that is emerging. The facilitator and the client jump into it together, in order to access dreaming experience.

Role-play theatre can be an effective way of enacting dreaming stories. The client's awareness determines the role or roles the client plays as the story unfolds. The client may wish to be actively involved in the drama, or may wish to take a more detached position, by taking the role of narrator. By taking the narrator role, the client may find a new chapter or scene that will resolve the drama, or experience new feelings and reactions. These may bring fresh insight and direction. Alternatively, resolution may be found in the creative unfolding of the story in song, poetry, dance, painting, or some other art-based activity, or in simply appreciating the story for its passion and fun.

If a client does not want to play an active role in a role-play drama, she may be more interested in directing the story, or in watching the roles interact, noticing what feelings or insights come from watching from the outside. She may find that she is fascinated by one role in particular, and want to jump into that role. Alternatively, she may find herself siding with a marginalized role, and have ideas about how that role should be played. If the client is shy to act things out, the facilitator can act out all the parts for her, or the drama can be told like a fairy tale, using stuffed animals, drawings or imaginary figures. Resolution is found in whatever experience is gained in watching, being, doing, or feeling, as the story unfolds.

Knowing when to drop a role-play

A role-play is a vehicle for amplifying experience. Once it has served its purpose, it needs to drop away. In this sense, a role-play is like a booster rocket, the bulky vehicle that lifts the payload (the tip of the rocket that holds all the essential intelligence) off the ground. The payload is the double signal that is unfolded to reveal its dreaming quality. As a booster rocket gets the payload off the ground and into space, a role-play helps to move a process from its consensus reality origins into dreaming experience. This is illustrated in the role-play in which the client, Vicky, accesses an "Alaskan" state of mind. At this point, Rita does not re-invoke the role-play, or try to keep the dialogue and interaction going. She drops the role-play and focuses on Vicky's internal experience. The second example, of Quincy and Angela, offers another example of dropping a role-play once it has served its purpose. Once Angela experiences her own authority, Quincy does not return to the initial dialogue.

In both role-plays, once the "payload" of the dreaming experience is achieved, the next step is to move forward into identification with that experience. Holding onto the initial role-play set-up tethers a dreaming experience to the primary process. This applies to all presenting issues, including relationship conflicts, body experiences, dreams, and other difficulties. If facilitator and client stay too close to the presenting issue and its initial context, they remain tied to an experience that is too

---

Exercise 5.2
Unfolding through Role-Play

Two people work together. Person A presents an issue and Person B facilitates using role-playing.

1. Person A identifies a central question in his or her life at the moment.
2. Person A and Person B together finds the polarities in this question, and distill the polarities so that the essential nature of each is expressed as a role.
3. Person B helps Person A enter the role that is furthest from his or her everyday identity by playing another role that is opposite to it.
4. While playing this role, Person B watches Person A's signals and tries to notice which role has an edge by looking for double signals such as incongruent statements, one role talking about another, and incomplete statements or movements.
5. Person A and Person B continue to unfold the role-play. Person B tries to unfold the role Person A is playing, by noticing and unfolding verbal and non-verbal signals, or switching roles.
6. Let the role-play fall away when a signal is followed to the point that something new emerges.

---

closely connected to the consensus world, and miss its inherent dreaming qualities.

Working with a critic in role-play

A "critic" is a marginalizing force, usually structured by a belief system, which renders an experience secondary. Role-plays often revolve around a marginalized experience, and a "critic" that is against it in some way. For instance, in the first role-play example, with Rita and Vicky, the role of "John," (the laid-back state) is marginalized by the "manager" role, which is critical of the laid-back state. There are various ways of working with a critical inner figure. A critic can be treated as an opponent with which to do battle, or it can be treated as a useful source of information, and then bypassed. As with any intervention, how to work with a critic is determined organically, by following signals.

Confronting a critic

In some situations, direct confrontation with a critic may be valuable. Where the critic is an abusive or oppressive figure connected with an individual's personal history or cultural background, it may be important to use role-play to enact a process of defending one's rights, or fighting and bringing down the critic. This may help a person to get in touch with strength or identity that has previously been marginalized, or bring awareness about dynamics of abuse, discrimination, or oppression.

Bypassing a critic

In some situations, engaging in a role-play with a critic is unnecessary and even counter-productive. The critic is an edge figure that can be bypassed. Stopping to interact with it inhibits a dreaming experience that is already happening. This is like trying to get over a fence into a meadow in which an ogre lives. In the meadow there are beautiful wildflowers and a creek. The ogre hangs out at the fence line, trying to stop anyone from getting into the meadow. One day, determined to get to the meadow, a person fights off the ogre, jumps the fence and reaches the meadow. But instead of wandering far into the meadow, smelling the flowers and sticking his toes in the creek, he spends the entire time at the fence. He keeps yelling at the ogre about his right to be there, even when the ogre is snoozing in the sun, posing no immediate threat.

Standing up against an oppressive critic can be a source of power and insight, but it may also get in the way of unfolding a secondary experience. A person's energy can become tied up in the battle, and the marginalized role does not get to experience itself, except in terms of what it is not. There is more to a role than what it stands against. Sometimes, more power is gained by experiencing unknown aspects of a role, than through short-term confrontation with a critic. A useful rule of thumb is to try to bypass a critic whenever possible. If it returns three times, interaction with the critic is necessary.

Overemphasizing confrontation with a critic

If a facilitator overemphasizes confrontation with a critic, or sides with the client against a critic, he may miss signals in the critic role that suggest what to unfold next. In addition, if the critic is engaged too early or too often, the critic may appear as opposition to a double signal, and the dreaming process may become defined by the critic before it has been fully experienced. This is illustrated in the following example.

A client comes to a therapy session complaining of fatigue. He sits down and droops in a chair, closing his eyes. As they start to work, a critical thought comes into the client's mind. He says, "Oh, I'm just being lazy. I should be working on myself, and instead, I'm just wasting my time." Here, the critic has defined his double signals. The signals that the critic calls "lazy" have not yet been unfolded. "Lazy" is merely a way in which the primary process labels something unknown. If the facilitator engages the critic in dialogue, the role-play will happen at the level of ideas and judgments.

The critic as a source of information

Often, when a critic comes up at an edge, it reveals information about a secondary process. In the language of the spy world, the critic is like a "mole," a source of information. For instance, in the first role-play, the manager criticizes "John" for being unprofessional. This criticism is actually a tip about how the role of "John" might develop. "Unprofessional" points to the client's need to relax and relate more to nature and less to professional pressures. Here, the content of the criticism, divorced from its critical style, contains valuable information about a secondary process. Noting what the critic says can help unfold a secondary process more deeply.

The critic as ally

The critic is often seen as the "bad guy." Facilitators sometimes think that their job is to promote self-esteem in their clients and protect them from critics that make them feel badly about themselves. They become activists against critics, forgetting that the critic is a part of a dreaming process, and contains energy and power that is needed by the client. For example, in Angela's case, the authoritarian critic represents her own inner authority and power. If the facilitator, Quincy, had taken a protective stance, he might have tried to protect from Angela from her critic. This protective stance could have disempowered Angela, because it would have cast her in the role of victim. As facilitators, it is helpful to remember that a client may or may not need to fight with, or gain protection from, a critical figure. An encounter with the power of a critic may be just what the client needs. A facilitator can help clients to be aware of their experiences during clashes with powerful figures, and to identify with the dreaming dimensions of the critical figures they encounter.

A simple guideline for working with critical figures in role play is to remember beginner's mind. Do not assume any prior knowledge about critical figures, or be pulled into defending the client from their judgment. Like any dream figure, they are a potential source of wisdom, and by keeping our minds open and curious, and following their signals without preconceived notions, we may be lucky enough to uncover their teachings.

Our different states of consciousness and styles of learning at any given moment determine how we access dreaming experiences. This chapter has shown how methods such as globalizing, shapeshifting and role play can be helpful in the process of unfolding, helping us to feel more at home in the world of non-ordinary experience. The next chapter introduces sentient methods of inhabiting the dreaming world.

Chapter 6

Sentient Paths to Dreaming Experience

The previous chapters have focused on unfolding "non-flickering" signals that can be felt, seen, heard and explored using sensory perception and second attention. In contrast, the flickering signals of sentient experience barely reach the threshold of sensory awareness, and do not translate readily into thought or words. Also called "pre-signals" or "flirts," flickering signals are like fireflies in the night, tiny traces of something that exists, yet barely perceivable in full physical form. They are visible one moment, gone the next, leaving us wondering whether they existed at all. In this chapter we will describe the sensory and feeling skills that help us to notice and unfold flickering signals. First, we will describe how flickering signals appear in the various channels. Then we will present three approaches to unfolding flickering signals, some skills and metaskills that are useful for working with sentient experience, and applications of sentient unfolding.

Channel experiences of flickering signals

Flickering signals occur in all channels. Visual flirts are fleeting images, quick fantasies, shapes, colors, textures or hues that catch one's attention for a fraction of a moment. An auditory flirt is a quiet, sudden, or small sound that catches the attention fleetingly. It may be a quality of voice, like a suggestion of hoarseness, breathiness, or wavering, a background melody that floats into the mind but is barely noticed, or a tiny sound in the environment. Flickering proprioceptive signals are sensations that barely cross the threshold of attention, such as a sudden or slight stirring, a tick, pulse, slight pressure, or twinge. Flicking movement signals are subtly felt tendencies toward motion or stillness. Flickering signals in the relationship channel are subtle feelings of attraction or aversion that flash across or shadow one's consciousness. They may also be coupled with movement tendencies, such as a slight hesitation, movement forward, or pulling back. World channel flirts include subtle, fleeting glimpses of environmental phenomena, or vaguely felt synchronicities.

Ways of unfolding flickering signals

One approach to unfolding flickering signals[38] involves noticing and unfolding flickering signals in marginalized perception. A second approach entails tracing a consensus reality or dreamland experience (such as a symptom, dreamfigure or relationship conflict) back to its pre-signal "root." A third approach involves training non-ordinary awareness to sense sentient experience before it manifests in everyday reality.

---

[38] Arnold Mindell, *Dreaming While Awake*, and *The Dreammaker's Apprentice: Using Heightened States of Consciousness to Interpret Dreams* (Charlottesville, VA: Hampton Roads Publishing Company, 2001).

Unfolding flickering signals in marginalized perception

This way of working with flickering signals involves using the subtle awareness of third attention to notice a signal and enter its world. Third attention is an unfocused awareness that is attracted by barely noticeable dreaming signals. It creates the kind of receptive mental state that allows flickering signals to come to conscious awareness. By meditating on a flickering signal that attracts the third attention, a person can identify its quality or energy. The next step is to shapeshift into it, by feeling into its feeling atmosphere and mindset, and imagining your way into its world-view, or by telling a story about it. This way of working with flickering signals is synaesthetic, in that it involves entering the world of the signal by altering one's state of consciousness, rather than using an analytic ability to break an experience down into discrete parts and channels. Exercise 6.1 gives a step-by-step guide to experiencing working with flickering signals in this way.

Unfolding backward to a sentient "root"

The non-flickering signals of experiences such as body symptoms, dream images, relationship conflicts, or moods can be unfolded forward into the world of dreamfigures. They can also be unfolded backward to their sentient "root," the dreaming tendency that gives rise to them. This begins with a particular experience, such as a body symptom. Using the diffuse awareness of third attention, an essential quality of the experience comes to mind. This quality is then expressed as a small body movement, such as a hand motion. The movement is slowed down and made smaller until it is almost imperceptible. Slowing the movement down and making it smaller are important because these counteract the tendency to use movement to override subtle proprioceptive experiences. The slower and more localized the movement, the more its quality becomes apparent. Next the movement is made even slower and smaller, until there is no more physical movement, only a movement trace in one's awareness. The core quality of the movement can

---

Exercise 6.1
Working with flickering signals

1. Find a comfortable spot. Sit or stand comfortably, letting your body relax.
2. Close your eyes, and take a few deep breaths. Let your mind relax and become open. Let your mind drift and wander. Allow subtle sensations and tendencies to come to your awareness. Do not try to focus on anything in particular.
3. Open your eyes very, very slowly. Notice the first visual signal that draws your attention (e.g. a shape, color, texture, shadow). It might be something you see, or something you only think you see.
4. Slowly unfold the experience by holding the fleeting impression that caught your attention in your awareness, staying with it, and letting it expand until you have a sense of its essential quality.
5. Allow a figure that represents that quality to come into your mind. Again, do not try to think of anything, hold your mind open and let a figure come up.
6. Let a story about the figure come into your mind, and stay with it until you feel it is done.

---

then be identified, and the energy that gave rise to the movement can be felt and described.

The difference between unfolding forward and unfolding backward can be illustrated by returning to a previous example. In the example of working with the dream image of a tree, the facilitator sees the tree in the signals of the client, and unfolds them "forward." The signals are encouraged to diversify from the visual channel into proprioceptive and movement channels, until the client has a multi-channeled experience of "treeness," and is able to identify "treeness" as a previously unfamiliar aspect of her personality.

In order to unfold the dream image backward to its sentient root, the client contemplates on the energy or quality that gave rise to the tree image. The facilitator might ask, "What is the energy of the tree before it becomes a tree?" Holding that energy in awareness, making a slight movement to represent it, and then slowing the movement down until it is an imperceptible tendency brings the client to a sentient experience of "treeness."

This approach to unfolding uses non-rational, non-analytical faculties. At its conclusion, the client has an intuitive sense of the significance of "tree" for her everyday life, without necessarily being able to articulate this fully. The example below illustrates working with a body symptom using unfolding techniques of signals and parts, and then working with the same symptom using the sentient method of finding the root of the symptom to enhance and deepen the experience.

SENTIENT UNFOLDING

A young man, Michael, comes to a counseling session complaining of job stress. He is a roofer who is attempting to start his own business. As he talks about the difficulties with starting his roofing business, he shifts uncomfortably in his chair. He says that his back and neck hurt from lifting heavy materials the previous day.

Both the job stress and the neck ache, as Michael describes them, are consensus reality experiences, which others could agree upon as reality.

The facilitator, Winston, asks Michael if he wants to work on the symptom, and Michael says that he does. He asks Michael to describe the experience of his neck ache, in terms of how it feels, what it's like, and so on. Michael says his neck pain feels like someone pinching the back of his neck, like a mother cat holding a kitten by the scruff of its neck. *This description provides information at the level of dream-land experience. The experience is subjective, described in terms of non-flickering signals in the visual and movement channels. It is non-consensual in the sense that others looking in on the conversation would not see the cat and kitten in Michael's neck.*

In order to unfold the experience further, Winston invites Michael to feel his neck again. Michael feels the ache, sees the image of the mother cat and kitten, and simultaneously feels himself being gently shaken by the mother cat. This is a spontaneous amplification of the initial symptom.

Next Winston asks Michael to focus on the feeling of being shaken by the scruff of the neck. Michael imagines a large hand, which picks him up by the scruff of his neck, and throws him around, like a limp rag doll. He suddenly smiles and says, "It feels really great to be hurled around like that!" He likes the experience of limpness, not having to do anything, and just being tossed around, and contrasts this with the tension he feels about starting his own business. Michael comments that the experience of being tossed around helped him realize how overwhelmed and uptight he has become, trying to go into business for himself. He sees that he has overly identified with a sense of responsibility in starting his own business, and the legal and financial details of becoming a small business owner have made him tense. The limpness in his symptom is just what he needs, an antidote for all his tension and worry. Although he still feels responsible, he realizes that tension and worry are not necessary. Shrugging his shoulders and smiling, he says, "We'll see. I'll do my best, and see what happens!"

Winston then asks Michael if he would like to go one step further. From Michael's signals (quiet voice, eyes closing slightly, or looking down), he has the sense that there is yet more to be experienced. He is interested in how the symptom might unfold if they worked on its sentient aspect.

Winston asks Michael to focus on the symptom again, and feel, if he can, the energy of the symptom in what it does to him. Michael says it is like a "grabbing." Winston asks Michael to make a small movement that expresses the grabbing energy. He holds a closed fist out in front of himself, as if holding something up. Winston then asks him to make the movement again, this time even more subtly, and to feel into the energy of that movement. Michael closes his eyes, and falls silent for a long time. After a long pause, he says, "It's like a...stopping". As he says this, Winston sees a tiny jerking backwards movement of his head and torso. He asks him to feel the jerking back energy, without making any movement. He then invites him to focus on its central quality or energy. Again, after a long pause, Michael, says "Nothing...Stopping. Just ...not doing anything. Empty, like nothing to be done."

Michael opens his eyes and Winston notices that Michael's normal state of consciousness has returned, because Michael is looking at him. Excitedly, Michael links this feeling to the mother cat and kitten from the previous work. "It's similar," he says, "but different. In the first experience, I felt the limp cat, felt myself being loose and easy. But this is different. This isn't even being easy-going. It's not doing anything. Easy-going is a way of going about what I have to do in my life. But this feels like there's nothing for me to do at all!"

In conclusion, Winston asks Michael one last question: "What is the attitude of not-doing? What does the world look like from the point of view of not-doing?" Michael thinks for a moment, with his eyes closed. Finally, he says, "Everything is perfect. Bureaucracy is good; working is good, not working is good!" Then he laughs. He has gotten to a deep, underlying spiritual understanding of life, an idea found in Zen teachings that "every day is a fine day." Using this method of "unfolding backwards," Michael is able to go more deeply into an experience, and tap into its sentient "root." This is initially an entirely subjective experience, one that is not expressed in words. A little later, he is able to formulate in words the significance of the experience for his everyday life.

Sensing sentient experience before it manifests in everyday reality

Mindell refers to the sentient force that moves individuals in their lives as the "intentional field." Similar to gravitational pull, or the dragon lines of the earth, this force is experienced as an "it," an impersonal intent that acts on individuals. It is not personal will-force. The intentional field is often experienced particularly strongly by people who are close to death.

Movement is particularly helpful in working with the intentional field. Postural tendencies and pre-movements can be sensed energetically in the body, allowing them to bring sentient experience into conscious awareness. Working with the intentional field begins with being still, allowing the body and mind to relax, and becoming aware of the slightest movement tendency. Then, it involves allowing oneself to be moved by the tendency, and letting that movement find expression as it is held in awareness. Exercise 6.2 provides a step-by-step exercise for this approach to accessing a sentient experience of the intentional field, using movement as a starting point. This method can also be used with sound, instead of movement, by beginning with a flickering signal of a sound, tone, or musical note, and allowing that to find expression in any way that emerges.

Skills for sentient work

Familiarity and ease with altered and non-verbal states of consciousness are particularly helpful for unfolding non-verbal signals and working effectively with sentient experience. Normal ways of talking, relating, thinking, or interpreting are less useful. The facilitator must be able to feel into and join in with an experience as it emerges.

In working with sentient experience, it is useful to amplify a client's experience from a state of meditative awareness. Here the facilitator uses her own synaesthetic experience to perceive and follow what is happening in the client. Synaesthetic experience is the experience of "just knowing," without being able to

Exercise 6.2
Accessing the intentional field

1. Find a comfortable spot. Stand with your arms hanging loosely at your side, legs slightly bent and relaxed.

2. Let your mind relax and become open. Do not focus on anything, just let your mind drift and lightly wander. Close your eyes, and feel your body. Let yourself become aware of different sensations, and slight, subtle tendencies. Do not try to notice anything, or focus on anything in particular. Let experiences tug gently at your awareness.

3. Ask yourself, what movement or posture is almost happening or tending to happen?

4. Let that tendency slowly emerge. Do not make it happen, but let it pull you.

5. Let it unfold, by following what is happening. Let the energy of the experience move you, feel it as you move. Take your time with this.

6. When you are ready to move out of the experience a little, ask yourself, "What is the energy of this experience like? What kind of time and space does it occupy? What is its essential quality?

7. What or who typifies this quality? Find a figure that matches its energy. Let the image emerge through feeling the energy. Don't try to think or focus too hard on finding an answer.

8. Allow yourself to feel into the figure and its state of mind. Become it, and experience its outlook on life, death, and eternity.

9. From this mindset, look at yourself in your everyday life. What do you notice? Is there a word, thought, advice or feeling that comes to you?

identify how or why. It is similar to an intuition or hunch, but is distinguished by the fact that it is experienced bodily. It is an "all-over" experience, which cannot be broken down into a single channel or reduced to a particular thought or idea. Questions that evoke this type of experience and inquire into it further include: "What is there, before this movement or image?" "What is its energy like?" "What experience is at the root of it?" or "What is its energy like, if nothing is against it?"

A facilitator needs to be skilled in recognizing signals that recommend sentient unfolding. Examples of such signals include difficulty in articulating an experience and long pauses or silence before responding. A facilitator can help a client go further into a sentient experience by using a special kind of "nonverbal language." This helps to train the client's awareness on sentient experience, temporarily leaving behind the thought patterns and concerns of everyday consciousness. It involves the use of words, phrases, sounds, and voice tone that do not require a response from the client. As a form of hypnotic induction, this way of communicating helps the client drop below the threshold of ordinary consciousness, and tap into the sentient realm.

In communicating with and supporting someone in a deeply altered state, a facilitator can adjust her voice tone and quality so that it is responsive to sentient experience. The voice is gentle, encouraging, and impersonal. It is conducive to an atmosphere that helps a person to get in touch with the essence of an experience. A low, quiet, resonant tone tends to help people go more deeply into an altered state. Sometimes a breathy, light tone is helpful. Examples of the use of voice tone in helping to access altered states are the resonant chanting of Tibetan and Medieval Christian monks, the rich tones of choral music, and the light, airy sounds of ambient music.

When people speak about sentient experience, their descriptions often sound vague and incomplete. They naturally tend to describe their experience poetically. Facilitators can also use poetic language to access and amplify sentient experience.

Poetic language is deliberately inexact. Rather than convey precise information, it evokes feelings, memories, and sensations. For example, a meadow might be described poetically as a "golden wave of wind," rather than "a field of grass." From an informational point of view, the poetic description is incorrect. But from a dreaming point of view, the description conveys a synaesthetic experience of the meadow. It helps a person experience it bodily, through the images, sensations, and atmosphere it evokes.

Metaskills for sentient work

The everyday mind is naturally trained to conceptualize, articulate, and translate symbols into meaning. In accessing sentient experience, a particular kind of edge is involved. This is the edge to leave the workings of the everyday mind and tap into states of awareness that cannot readily be expressed in words. Metaskills that are particularly helpful in working with sentient experience center on the ability to shift from one state of consciousness to another.

Patience

Working with sentient experience can be slow and painstaking, and requires patient encouragement. A facilitator needs to encourage a client to go deep down below the threshold of normal consciousness, and sense subtle and inexpressible tendencies. Such experiences are generally not encouraged or supported in everyday life, and people may take a long time to tune into them. Patience is more than a virtue here. It gives a client the time to feel, sense and notice, without the pressure of having to know. A patient facilitator trusts the meandering nature of a process, and the solutions that arise out of it, letting go of therapeutic and solution-focused agendas, and leaving behind the belief that a particular outcome must be achieved.

Stepping out of the way

Mystics, clairvoyants and spiritual teachers frequently say that they themselves do nothing; they are a vehicle for a divinity, spirit or greater consciousness that works through them. They view their task as to channel a greater wisdom than their own, by stepping out of the way. In working with sentience, a facilitator needs to embrace this attitude as well. He feels that he is doing nothing, but is being moved by the intentional field that moves everything. The belief that the facilitator is a vehicle for the dreaming process, and that personal effort does not effect change, is particularly important in working with sentient experience.

Lucidity and cloudedness

In *Dreaming While Awake*, Mindell defines lucidity as: "awareness of sentient experience, which precedes everything you think, see, hear, and do. ... When you are lucid, you sense tendencies as well as actualities."[39] Lucidity is a detached, diffuse, state of mind that is essential for working with sentience. It is adept at catching the merest suggestions of experience. Mindell uses a musical analogy to convey its particular quality: "Consciousness involves writing or knowing the notes of a song, while lucidity is awareness of the feeling background that gave rise to the song."[40] Mindell also refers to lucidity as "cloudedness," to emphasize its loose, relaxed, not-knowing quality. Like peripheral vision, it is not focused on any one object or point of reference. It does not involve working, searching for meaning, or trying to achieve, understand, or clarify.

---

[39] Mindell, *Dreaming While Awake*, 36.
[40] Ibid, 69.

Applications of sentient unfolding

Feedback guides every decision about how to unfold a process. The choice to use a sentient approach, like any other, is suggested by a client's signals. Here are some examples.

Aversion to confrontation and conflict

Signals that stem from a fear of confrontation or conflict, helplessness, or despondence may recommend sentient unfolding methods. A client may move away from an edge, instead of showing interest or excitement, or there may be a lack of energy in a client's presentation or in the general atmosphere of a session. Because sentient experience does not involve working with polarities, confrontation with difficult edges is reduced. A sentient approach to unfolding can be a nourishing and loving way to address inner and outer conflicts.

Chronic symptoms, stress and fatigue

Sentient unfolding methods counter the stress of pushing and striving. Because they adopt a non-verbal approach and access altered states of consciousness, they give the body a chance to experience "non-doing." This may be useful for someone who suffers from chronic symptoms, or stress-related physical difficulties. Overwhelming body experiences, such as fatigue, pain, and stress, can diminish a person's capacity to focus and relate. Signals that might invite a sentient approach to unfolding include looking down, sighing, spacing out, talking slowly, pausing a lot, or trailing off at the end of a sentence.

Moods and depression

Some moods or prolonged affective states, like depression, respond well to sentient work. Sometimes a form of mild chronic depression, felt as an unfulfilled longing, melancholy or a sense of emptiness,[41] can indicate that a person needs to access deeper or subtler experiences. This is suggested in signals such as an uncertainty or lack of interest in what to work on, hopelessness, heavy sighs or noisy exhalation, a slouching or slumping posture, prolonged downward glances, and frequent pauses or unfinished sentences.

Sometimes, an inability to live one's hopes or dreams brings bitterness or despair. When this is the case, a client's speech may include words that suggest regret or a fixed view of reality, such as "if only," "once," "always," "ever" or "never." Other moods may be characterized by prolonged anger and resentment. For example, a client may be caught in the grip of trying to change something (a relationship, an organization, or community, for example), which looks unlikely to change.

Use of sentient methods for working with depression is illustrated in the following example, in which a client, Sushila, comes to see a therapist, Leo, because she feels trapped in her life.

SENTIENT WORK WITH DEPRESSION

Sushila has always wanted to be an artist but has never felt able to let go of her job and financial responsibilities. She feels bound by an obligation to support her parents in their old age, and is also partly responsible for financially supporting her partner's children. When Leo encourages her to change her work, or tries to address practical matters such as money, lifestyle and family relationships, Sushila only becomes more depressed. She sighs, leans back in her chair, and expresses a longing for something to happen that would make her life feel more creative. Leo notices that her signals indicate a pattern of high and low dreaming: a high dream of becoming an artist, followed by a low dream, hopelessness, when the dream does not come true.

---

[41] For further discussion on the connection between depression and sentience, see Rhea Shapiro, "Noticing the Spirits in Everyday Life: Process Work as Spiritual Practice and Antidote to Mild Chronic Depression," *The Journal of Process-oriented Psychology*, Vol.8, 2, Winter 2001, 75-83.

Leo sees that Sushila's signals recommend a sentient approach to unfolding. He works with the sentient experience behind Sushila's dream of being an artist. Leo asks Sushila to imagine the artist she wants to be. Sushila says that she sees a wildly dressed woman, wearing a leopard-print silk scarf, bright red knee-high boots, a leather skirt, and a shaggy sheepskin vest. As she describes the image, she also makes distinctive movements, so Leo asks her to bring the artist she is imagining into her movements and posture as well. Sushila sits up straight in her chair, and makes flamboyant, dramatic, directive movements with her arms, tossing her head back. Leo then asks her to make the movements smaller, until they become one tiny gesture. Sushila makes a slight waving motion with her hand, and at the same time, lifts her chin as if she is tossing her head back ever so slightly. Leo asks her to feel the quality of her movements and posture, without moving at all. Sushila closes her eyes and finally, after a long minute, she says, "Mhmm, it feels like lightness, freedom. Almost like flying ...cloud-like..." She stops speaking, and continues to experience it for a little while longer.

While Sushila is still immersed in the experience, Leo asks her to imagine a figure that represents the quality of her head movement. She opens her eyes slowly and says, "It's like a queen or tall, regal bird, someone who is utterly free to fly wherever she wants." Leo encourages her to look at the world with that free state of mind, and then to look back at herself in her everyday life. "From this perspective," he asks, "what do you notice?" Sushila closes her eyes and sits perfectly still, with her chin up, looking regal and serene. After a few minutes, she smiles. "It's not about doing anything different," she says. "Being an artist means being artistic, unusual, spontaneous. I'm so predictable and boring," she says, bursting into laughter. "Even this problem, of wanting to do more art, I approach it in a profoundly non-artistic way!"

In this example, use of a sentient method of unfolding produces a "hyperspatial" solution: one that arises out of an altered state of consciousness. Hyperspatial solutions add another dimension to everyday consciousness, which tends to view the world from a dualistic point of view. Sometimes, everyday problems cannot be solved by the everyday mind making a choice between possibilities, such as: "Stay with my partner or leave?" "Take the job or not?" "Go back to school or not?" The sentient perspective views every possibility as already existing. Present problems, feelings, mind-sets all spring from undifferentiated experience. By accessing this experience using sentient methods, moods related to problems and choices in the everyday world are relieved, and ways forward become clear.

Addictions

Like moods, addictions may be attempts to find sentient solutions to apparently intractable problems. The presence of an addiction may signal that a hyperspatial solution may be required. Using sentient methods to work on addictions may help a person to access the altered states of consciousness they are seeking in their use of a particular substance, without harmful side effects. An example of using a sentient approach to working with an addiction follows.

SENTIENT WORK WITH ADDICTION

Dionne, a drug and alcohol counselor, is working with a client, Wes, on his marijuana addiction. Wes has been a daily marijuana user for over twenty years. His typical pattern is to get furious with himself every so often, and then quit, cold turkey, right away. His resolve holds for about three days, and then he gets depressed and anxious. Finally, he feels so low that he can no longer use discipline or resolve to stop himself, and he starts smoking again. When Wes and Dionne work together on the addiction, Wes describes his state of mind when he is "stoned" as blissful, a place without conflict or stress. He feels happy and at peace with himself. He contrasts how he feels when he is stoned with his attitude to himself when he quits smoking. Then he feels self-critical, and angry with himself for his weakness. He uses this anger as way of "disciplining himself" into quitting. He flips between the self-loving state he experiences when he is using marijuana, and the harsh, tough-love attitude of quitting.

Dionne thinks that quitting will never stick if it is just an impulsive reaction against marijuana and being weak. In fact, Wes's harshness seems to be a catalyst for relapse, since it triggers a need for self-love that using marijuana satisfies. Thinking that self-love must be a cornerstone in Wes's process, Dionne decides to try and use the self-love state as a new pattern for quitting. She asks Wes to recall what it is like be "stoned," and carefully watches his body signals. Wes closes his eyes, breathes deeply, and leans back in his chair. A slight smile plays at his lips. "Ahhh," he says. "This is perfect. No worries whatsoever." Joining him by matching his signals, Dionne goes into that mindset with Wes. They sit quietly, enjoying the feeling of ease and calm. Without changing her tone or tempo, Dionne asks Wes, "Hmm, what a lovely peaceful state. What kind of quitting method would match this peaceful, easy going state?" She lets the question hover, watching to see what kind of reply Wes's somatic signals might give. Wes keeps his eyes closed, and a little smile appears on his face. "Well," he says, speaking slowly, "it certainly wouldn't be stressful. In fact, it'd probably be so subtle, I wouldn't even notice I was quitting!"

Following this hyperspatial recommendation from the altered state of consciousness, Dionne and Wes come up with a subtle and non-stressful method for Wes to quit smoking marijuana. Dionne asks him, "How long will it take for you to quit, in such a way, that you'd hardly feel it?" Wes thinks about this for a while, and then says, "Maybe nine months." Whereas his previous quitting method was an impulsive decision, made in the throes of self-disgust, the new approach will take months. He can smoke marijuana as much as he likes for the first month, and then taper off slowly over the next eight months. In the nine months that follow, Dionne and Wes look at many other areas of Wes's life, and discover where harshness makes him crave marijuana. They also work on reducing the triggers for using marijuana, by bringing a more blissful and self-loving attitude to other areas of his life.

Sentient approaches to unfolding are useful when the problem itself involves an altered state, as in an addiction. Wes's use of marijuana is an attempted sentient method. Being stoned is a gentle and soothing way of way of accessing the self-loving, relaxed state Wes lacks. The stoned state, however, is insufficient. It prevents Wes from truly reaching a gentle, self-loving state because it also diminishes his awareness. Using a sentient approach to working on Wes's problem enables him to become aware of the state he is seeking in his use of marijuana, and use that awareness to tailor a plan for quitting that is consistent with that state.

The experiences we have in dreaming states of consciousness are profound. They are a type of non-cognitive learning. By experiencing new states of mind, attitudes and parts of ourselves, our sense of self expands enormously. Yet, we often want cognitive understanding and help to live this more fully in our every day lives and share it with others. The next two chapters introduce edge work, which helps us identity with new parts of ourselves, and live them in our work, relationships, and communities.

Chapter 7

At the Edge of the Unknown

On any journey, there are moments of uncertainty, doubt, or self-criticism. We suffer doubt about where to go next. We may be afraid or lonely. The joy and exhilaration of moving forward into new territory is matched by the stress and fear that are also par for the course. On a personal growth journey, any and all of these experiences may arise as the everyday identity encounters the unknown, and parts of the personality divide and conflict around whether to go forward and which way to go next. Such experiences happen at the "edge," the boundary between the everyday identity and unknown experience. In this chapter, we will explain the Process Work concept of the edge, and describe how to recognize edge signals. We will explore ways of following signals at an edge, and other edge work interventions. Finally, we will discuss some of the metaskills that are helpful when working with edges.

What is an edge?

An edge is a point of contact between the everyday identity, and an unknown, or dreaming experience. It is the boundary between the primary process (everyday identity) and the secondary process (emergent identity). Edges are also dynamic moments of transition, in which a known way of understanding oneself is disrupted and transformed by something new. A primary process marginalizes certain experiences, thereby creating an edge. Once secondary experiences are brought into everyday awareness, they become primary, rendering other experiences secondary, and creating new edges.

In the early stages of following a process, the edges that arise are sometimes called "micro-edges." These are momentary or short-term experiences connected with the various stages of unfolding (see Box 8.1). Initially, there is an edge to focus on something secondary. The everyday mind is accustomed to its reliance on first attention, and may be reluctant or afraid to shift into another way of seeing and knowing. Once this edge is crossed, and attention has shifted to something secondary, more edges arise as signals are amplified and folded. Edges may come up at various points in the amplification and unfolding process, such as letting go of experience in occupied channels, and moving into experiences in unoccupied channels. Changing from conceptual, verbal or visual modes of experience into body-centered (proprioceptive and kinesthetic) experience often brings up edges.

In the later stages of unfolding, "macro-edges" arise. These are related to identifying with dreamfigures, and integrating dreaming experience into everyday life in the long term.

Recognizing an edge

Recognizing an edge is a first step in working with edges. Edges can be found in verbal and nonverbal signals, and in changes in energy, atmosphere or relational intensity between facilitator and client. Energetic changes might include a drop in

---

Box 7.1
Stages in unfolding edges

1. Edge to focus on something secondary (switch from first attention to second or third attention).
2. Edge to amplify a secondary experience by adding or switching channels, entering an unoccupied channel.
3. Edge to identify with the mindset of a dreamfigure, and integrate it in the short-term.
4. Edge to integrate a secondary experience into one's daily life.

---

energy (boredom, dissociation, spacey-ness, or withdrawal), or a sudden burst of energy, accompanied by a profusion of signals. These might include embarrassed laughter, giggling, sweating, fidgeting, or holding the breath.

Some edges are created by disavowal; known aspects of identity are disliked or rejected. Often this is due to family or cultural beliefs, or prior negative experiences. This type of edge is characterized by strong opinions, feelings, and behavior such as nervousness, embarrassment, giggling or freezing. Typical verbal signals around this type of edge are: "Oh, I could never do that! That's awful, inflated, hurtful, stupid..." or "If I did that, I would be..." Another type of edge is created by complete lack of knowledge. No experience, no model, has left a footprint, as in untrammeled snow. There is no path forward, no prior experience to rely on. This type of edge is characterized by blankness, a generalized fear of the unknown, and spacey or trance-like behavior.

General clues about the presence of edges are found in how a client speaks and the manner in which information is presented. These include holes or gaps in information, abrupt channel changes, incomplete sentences or movements, and repeating information (cycling). Dissociation, indicated by missing information, absence of emotion, or lack of reaction, may also indicate that an edge is present. Belief systems that are stated without any meta-comment suggest the presence of an edge, as do synchronicities, accidents, paranormal experiences, and some physical symptoms or reactions.

Finally, the experience of the facilitator is also an important factor in recognizing an edge. If a facilitator finds herself losing track of the conversation, getting lost, feeling nervous, uncomfortable or embarrassed, or not knowing what to do next, this may reflect an edge in the client's process. A facilitator who becomes over-identified with a particular outcome or part of the process, or who feels pressure to achieve something, may also be picking up the presence of an edge.

Metaskills of edge work

Feeling attitudes are particularly important in working with edges. Metaskills create the kind of atmosphere that holds an unfolding process in moments of turbulence and uncertainty. Here are some examples of attitudes and beliefs that can guide a facilitator in working with edges.

Valuing constraint and creativity

Valuing an edge as a site of creative potential is a helpful metaskill in working with edges. At an edge, as in art, there is constraint and creativity. An artist's canvas imposes the limits of two-dimensionality. A writer is constrained by the limits of verbal expression, a sculptor by the properties of clay or stone. Yet, these media are also vehicles for innovation and creativity. Similarly, an edge is both limiting and creative. It holds a process back, yet it also has great potential. The unique expression of an individual emerges out of an interaction with an edge.

Encountering fate

Edges expose deeply held beliefs about life, death, and change, and provoke self-reflective questions such as: "How do I relate to the unknown in myself and others?" or "What do I find out

---

Box 7.2
Recognizing Edges

1. Look for energetic changes:
   - Embarrassed laughter, giggling, sweating, fidgeting, a profusion of signals
   - Energy drops: boredom, dissociation, spacey-ness, withdrawal
   - Energy comes up suddenly, in a big outburst
   - Holding breath
2. Look for holes or gaps in information:
   - Sudden channel changes with incongruent patterns and contents
   - Incomplete sentences, movements
   - Holes, missing words, trailing off sentences
   - Cycling (repeating information)
   - Dissociation: missing information, absence of emotion, or lack of reaction
3. Unexplained information:
   - Belief systems or value systems stated without meta-comment
   - Synchronicities, accidents, paranomral experiences
   - Physical symptoms or reactions
4. Faicilitator's experience:
   - Losing track of the conversation, getting lost
   - Nervousness, discomfort, embarassment
   - Not knowing what to do next
   - Feeling identified with one outcome or part
   - Feeling pressured to get somewhere

---

about myself when I come across an obstacle, or something scary?" The metaskill of "encountering fate" is based on the belief that edge work is about developing one's relationship to fate or something bigger than the individual. The client's relationship to the unknown is central here, and the facilitator's task is to help the client with this relationship, rather than to try and ensure that a particular edge is crossed.

Nowhere to go

The metaskill of "nowhere to go" contradicts the belief that it is a facilitator's responsibility to help a person to cross an edge. This metaskill is based in the belief that the process itself, rather than the facilitator's interventions, resolves hesitations and resistance. A client's signals show how the edge can be negotiated, both in terms of strategy and timing.

The metaskill of "nowhere to go" is a form of "wu-wei," or not-doing. It involves trusting in nature and the wisdom of a client's process, rather than relying on a facilitator's skills or a client's willingness. Clients can feel pushed or criticized by facilitators who feel that edge work is largely their responsibility. The self-importance behind this identification as a change-agent may be disturbing to the client's process, and may also make a client feel she has to do something or get somewhere, in order for the work (and the facilitator) to be successful.

An edge is a fertile place for learning and growth. It brings encounters with personal history, critics, fear, and other inner and outer experiences, which sharpen the second attention, and develop the ability to focus on unknown experience. With the metaskill of "nowhere to go," a facilitator is primarily interested in the awareness generated by an encounter with an edge, rather than the goal of getting anywhere.

Working with edges

Working with edges centers on signal awareness, feedback and metaskills. A client's signals at an edge always provide information about how to work with the edge and the direction in which to proceed. In particular, edge work is shaped by how a client encounters an edge. Sometimes the person experiences something unknown from the viewpoint of her everyday self. Edge work here involves helping the everyday mind to open up and make room for disavowed experience. At other times, the encounter is a clash between opposing beliefs or cultural influences. Here, edge work involves working with the experiences and beliefs that structure the edge. And sometimes, the person works with the edge by jumping over it, and allowing the experience itself to create a change.

Approaching an edge from the primary process

Approaching an edge from the vantage point of the normal identity is like peering over the edge of a cliff, and saying, "Holy cow! How am I ever going to get across that?" A facilitator can engage, support and encourage the primary process in a number of ways.

Interventions include encouraging and supporting a person to explore the edge, and even pushing gently while attending carefully to feedback. Reframing an experience can also be helpful. A facilitator can to talk to a client about a secondary process, describing it in terms that make it seems less negative, frightening or strange, and exploring what makes it feel so difficult. Dreaming into and expanding the client's knowledge of the secondary process by telling a story about it can help to create a feeling of detachment or safety, and create patterns for the experience over the edge. Enacting the secondary experience and the edge against it "outside" the person, using props, toys, or objects, are also helpful for this, since a client can observe or direct what is happening without feeling too exposed or vulnerable.

The following dialogue illustrates working with an edge from the primary process. It expands the example presented in Chapter Seven, in which a client, Vicky, works with a facilitator, Rita, on a dream about Alaska. The dialogue picks up at the point where Vicky begins to play the role of "John," a laid-back person at work who reminds her of Alaska. Vicky comes to an edge when Rita asks her to identify with the more laid-

---

Box 7.3
Approaching an edge from the primary process

- Support the person to go explore or go over the edge.Lovingly encourage, or even push a bit, while watching the client's feedback.
- Reframe the experience; talk to the primary process about the secondary process,describing it in terms that reduce its frightening, negative or marginal quality.
- Discuss the secondary experience with the primary process; find out what makes the new experience so frightening or difficult.
- Dream into and expand the client's knowledge of the secondary process. Dreaming into it, or telling a story about it creates patterns and models for the experience over the edge.
- Enact the secondary experience and edge against it "outside" the person, using props, toys, or objects, so the person can observe or direct what is happening.

---

back part of herself that the dreamfigures "Alaska" and "John" represent.

WORKING WITH AN EDGE
FROM THE PRIMARY PROCESS

RITA: If Alaska could be represented by a figure, who could represent that quality?

VICKY: Well, actually John, the guy in the dream who included me. He's kind of a slob, somewhat rough. He reminds me of Alaska.

RITA: Could you be him? Show me how he relates.

VICKY: Oh no. I couldn't do that. He's a real slob. I'm not at all like him!

Notice this is an edge from the primary process side: Vicky is looking at something on the other side of her edge, from the viewpoint of her everyday identity.

RITA: Oh, well, sometimes sloppy is good; it's relaxed, not so uptight. *She speaks to the primary process, trying to reframe sloppiness as "relaxed," and encouraging Vicky at the edge.*

VICKY: Well, if I did that, I'd never get any work done. You have to be professional in my line of work! *Her feedback shows that reframing is not helpful, but it suggests that a belief system is in place, indicated by the statement: "You have to be professional."*

RITA: Well, can you imagine some fairy tale figure or animal who is sloppy? What kind of figure might also be sloppy? *Her intervention bypasses the belief system. She decides instead to dream over the edge indirectly. At this point, arguing with the belief system of the primary process would mean arguing about a double signal, since Vicky hasn't yet unfolded the experience of "slob." Rita tries first to unfold "sloppy" indirectly by associating to it, allowing Vicky's imagination to run with it, without encountering the edge directly.*

VICKY: Well, as you said that, the image of Dopey in the Seven Dwarves just came to mind!

RITA: Dopey? Which one is he? *Even though she probably knows which dwarf Dopey is, she is more interested in Vicky's subjective description.*

VICKY: You know, the little one whose pants are always just a bit drooping, and well, he's kind of cute, but goofy, kind of out of it.

Dopey unfolds "sloppy" with less threat to the primary process. The speed with which Vicky imagines Dopey is a sign of positive feedback.

RITA: How does Dopey behave?

VICKY: Oh well, he's just easy going, goes along with all the other dwarves to the mines every day, but he's not overly concerned with how much coal he'll get. He just likes hanging out with his mates. *She laughs.* He's friendly and fun!

Vicky and Rita have found a path over the edge in Vicky's signals. They unfolded the "John" figure without having to negotiate the belief system against sloppiness. The dream figure of John is a friendly, fun quality that is needed by the dreamer in her everyday life, especially in relationship to her work.

Working with beliefs at an edge

Sometimes edge work involves a clash between tightly held beliefs. This is often a turbulent experience, bringing feelings of insecurity, fear, nervousness, and embarrassment. Like stepping through an airport security system, an alarm goes off at the threshold of the new experience, and fearful and critical reactions come up. This type of edge experience calls for interventions that deal with belief systems, personal history, feelings, emotions, and altered states.

The technique of "forbidding" is a useful way of intervening at this type of edge. Forbidding involves amplifying resistance to a secondary process, and can be done in a number of ways (see Box 8.4). One way involves representing the critic, or belief system that is in conflict with the secondary process, by enacting the conflict in a role play, or by discussing the pros and cons of the secondary identity or experience. Resistance work using movement (for example, pushing against something that represents the critic), can also help people feel their power and negotiate difficult edges. When the critic is fleshed out in this way, it can help the client to justify herself more strongly, or be more detailed, exact, or confident in taking the next step forward.

Forbidding can also be done paradoxically or with humor. The facilitator may encourage the client by doubting facetiously, for instance, "No! You? You could never do that!" while winking and smiling. Being challenged like this, with humor and love, can sometimes give the client an extra dose of

---

Box 7.4

Using Forbidding as an Intervention at the Edge

- Challenging the person paradoxically
- Forbidding the experience by representing a critic or edge figure
- Using resistance with movement to help the person feel the intensity of the secondary process
- Finding the ghost figures, the other parts of the experience, and what the person is moving towards, away from, or reacting to

---

courage, helping him to believe in himself, or take a risk. This technique should be employed with skill and careful attention to the client's feedback, and requires a good working relationship between client and therapist. Otherwise, the client might be hurt or misunderstand the intervention.

Interventions right at an edge often deal with aspects of personal history. Sometimes people need to remember past experiences, feeling and appreciating what they have been through. Sometimes it is important to spend time with a particular experience or story, revisiting it, or healing its various components. People may also need to negotiate with cultural, ancestral and familial "ghosts," whose ways and beliefs they are leaving behind.

Finding out what figure in the person's past is stopping them from going forward, telling a story about it, and unfolding the reaction, emotion, or part of the story that is incomplete, are all ways of finishing unfinished business. Sometimes the edge is vague, or it is unclear what or who is stopping the client from going forward, and edge work may involve taking the time to carefully help the client become conscious of a "ghost figure," or experience buried deep in the client's history.

When working at the edge, it is sometimes possible to bypass a critic or edge figure altogether and access the secondary process directly, or indirectly though an altered state of consciousness. Following a trance-like experience can be helpful to dream a person over an edge, and access an altered state of consciousness where valuable experience and information can be gained before going further. Alternatively, a facilitator can help the client to step outside his everyday identity by inviting him to imagine being drunk, an alien, a child, crazy or free, in order to access new experiences and insights.

In the remainder of this chapter, we will revisit the example of Rita and Vicky, in order to explore different ways of working with edges. The first example shows how the work might continue if Rita worked with the belief system behind Vicky's edge to being more laid-back.

WORKING WITH A BELIEF SYSTEM AT THE EDGE

RITA: If Alaska could be represented by a figure, who could represent that quality?

VICKY: Well, actually John, the guy in the dream who included me. He's kind of a slob, somewhat rough. He reminds me of Alaska.

RITA: Could you be him? Show me how he relates.

VICKY: Oh no. I couldn't do that. He's a real slob. I'm not at all like him!

The strong affect that accompanies the statement "I'm not at all like him," suggests an edge.

RITA: Really? Well, maybe there's something good about being slobby, no?

Rita first attempts to reframe the edge, talking to the primary about the secondary process.

VICKY: *She looks upset.* No, uggh, I hate slobby people. *She frowns and looks down.*

It looks like she is thinking or feeling something, maybe having a memory. Her verbal signals ("I hate slobby people") sounds as though she is referring to something, or someone she knows.

RITA: Why? What's wrong with slobby people? Looks like you're thinking or feeling something about that.

VICKY: Ugh, yeah. *She shakes head, and seems lost in thought.* My whole family was like that. Slobs. Especially my father. You know, they were alcoholics, and well, it was just a real difficult scene growing up. I was the only one who cleaned the house, the only one that did anything responsible. The lot of them, they were just hopeless.

RITA: Well, that's impressive. Look how professional you are now, and what you had to overcome to get here today. Congratulations!

VICKY: *She smiles wryly.* Yeah, it wasn't easy!

RITA: I bet. You've worked awfully hard. How'd you do it?

Rita is following Vicky into a story from her past. Because it arises at the edge, something in that story needs to be focused on.

VICKY: Well, no choice really. You know, I remember the day I left home. God, I thought that day would never come. I feel like I held my breath for 17 years, just waiting for a chance to leave.

RITA: What happened on that day?

VICKY: Well, even though nothing in my experience had shown me that anyone cared one whit about me, I still stupidly hoped or dreamed that as I drove away, they would all come and say goodbye! Or, at least wave. *She gives an ironic, wistful smile.* Isn't that stupid? I grew up in the most dysfunctional family ever, for 17 years, and there I was, leaving home, hoping this picture-perfect Mom and Dad would proudly wave off their daughter as she left home. *She shakes her head in disbelief. The story of the proud parent is happening in the moment, in the telling of the story.*

RITA: Well, I guess you dreamt it because you hoped for it. What would that proud parent have said if she or he were there then?

The edge brings up unfinished business. "Then" is now. The "slob" is the part of Vicky that does not praise her, does not notice her accomplishments, and probably is one of the reasons that she works so hard and strives to be so professional. It is a "ghost," a missing part that she needs to develop. This example shows that crossing some edges may require crossing other edges first. Vicky has unfinished business to attend to. To become a "slob" in the positive sense of being able to be her natural self, relax, and not work so hard, requires that she go back and pick up some pieces of her past that need finishing. In particular she needs to develop a "parenting" attitude, with which she can notice and appreciate herself.

Dreaming together over the edge

Sometimes, a client can slip directly into a secondary process, without encountering much resistance at an edge. She passes straight through the security system, without setting off any bells and buzzers, and finds herself in a new world. To explore the new terrain, it is helpful to have company, allies and fellow travelers. Interventions that directly amplify the secondary process without engaging a primary process or critic at the edge model the quality, language and expressions of the secondary process. The facilitator joins the client, using movement, role-play, and other types of intervention.

A facilitator can amplify a secondary process by role-playing with a client, either symmetrically (becoming the same figure as the client) or complementarily (taking a position complementary to the figure adopted by the client). An example of a symmetrical way of doing this is for both facilitator and client to become "John," and relax together. Finding a fantasy figure who models the secondary experience on the others side of the edge, and then becoming the figure is another way of dreaming further into it. A facilitator can encourage a client to use creative imagination to dream into a secondary experience, build it out, and explore and discover all of its dimensions and

---

Box 7.5
Working with the dreaming process over the edge

- Acting out the parts or events of the new experience. For instance, a client and facilitator could role-play different parts.
- Finding a fantasy figure that represents a secondary process, and then becoming the figure.Encouraging a client to use creative imagination to dream into an experience, and discover all of its dimensions and facets. This includes dreaming about the new identity, and how it looks in everyday life.
- Use hands-on techniques. If the person gives clear permission, a facilitator can use movement and bodywork interventions to explore a non-verbal experience. Pressure, sculpting, amplification of breathing, gentle shaking, or other techniques can deepen the client's experience.

---

facets. This includes dreaming about the figure, its lifestyle and worldview, and how it might relate to the client's everyday life.

Hands-on techniques are useful if a client gives a facilitator direct and unambiguous permission to use touch in an unfolding process. A facilitator can use movement and bodywork interventions to more fully explore a non-verbal experience. The facilitator can use pressure, sculpting, amplification of breathing, gentle shaking, or other techniques to help deepen the client's experience.

All of these interventions depend on a facilitator's congruence, or ability to match the energy, intensity, tone, and quality of that which is being unfolded. A facilitator must pick up the energy and quality of the secondary process, in the intervention itself. This is illustrated below, returning once again to the example of Rita and Vicky's work together.

EDGE WORK THROUGH PICKING UP
THE QUALITY OF THE SECONDARY PROCESS

VICKY: *Coming out of the role of the manager:* It's funny, being that woman for some reason makes me think of Alaska!

RITA: Why, what about Alaska?

VICKY: Well, in a way, it's like the opposite. It's so, so.... wild and loose! *She relaxes her posture, slouches in her chair, and makes a waving gesture with her hand.* People say it's the last frontier, lawless, and rugged. It's just like...well, nature. No laws, no ... tight little circles, or ranking people. It's the wilderness and it doesn't care about people's social standing. If you survive, that's rank!

   Seeing her signals talking about Alaska, Rita sees that the Vicky has slipped over the edge, and is entering an "Alaska" frame of mind, not just talking about it.

RITA: *She joins the client over the edge by putting her feet up on the stool, leaning back and folding her hands behind her head.* Yeah, loose and lawless! I like that!

VICKY: *She laughs at the alliteration, "loose and lawless."* Yeah, loose, lawless and laid back! *Both of them laugh and lean back in their chairs.*

RITA: Yeah, laid back, lawless, loose, and letting it all hang out! It feels like we're two old-timers just shootin' the breeze on the front porch. *Rita dreams into the experience, letting her imagination unfold the client's signals further.*

VICKY: Yup, two old codgers, chewing tobacco and shootin' the breeze. Nothin' to do, nowhere to go!

Vicky's feedback to Rita's amplifying the secondary experience directly is positive. Vicky immediately enters into an imaginative state, dreaming the story further. There is no thinking about the experience, interpreting it, or reframing. The experience is its own integration. She has a full experience of that state of mind, and through living it out, integrates it.

Edges and Levels of Awareness

Many issues cycle around the same edge. Each time, the edge is approached in a new way, bringing new perspectives. An edge may be viewed differently, depending on whether it is seen from the perspective of consensus reality, dreamland or sentience. From a consensus reality viewpoint, edges appear as outer obstacles. There are concrete reasons or material circumstances that prevent a person from living life in a certain way, or fulfilling certain desires or goals. If this is the case, clients need help to make changes. They need information, education, steps, or concrete support. There is also an inner component to an edge experience, but the way of negotiating the edge at a consensus reality level is to learn something new, get outer help with something, or enlist friends and support systems.

From a dreamland viewpoint, negotiating an edge involves interaction with dream figures. The edge appears as an inner dynamic, rather than as an outer obstacle. The inner dynamic makes the outer obstacle feel overwhelming. Here clients need help to engage with parts of themselves that hold them back.

From a sentient viewpoint, there is no edge to cross because there is no marginalization at the sentient level; there is only dreaming experience. Unlike dreamland and consensus reality approaches to edge work, sentient edge work does not require the sacrifice of personal history or identity. Edge interventions at the sentient level drop the client more deeply into a dreaming experience. Sentient dreaming at an edge involves finding a hyperspatial solution, one from another state of consciousness. It involves dreaming a solution, rather than working on one.

Describing edges in terms of levels of awareness implies that edges are perceived at one level or another, when in reality, all three ways of perceiving edges are intertwined. All three levels of awareness are useful in edge work; an edge is simultaneously an outer problem, an inner dynamic, and no problem at all!

Three levels of awareness in edge work

The following examples illustrate three different ways of working with the same edge. Each example illustrates the use of a different level of awareness, as indicated by the client's signals. A facilitator, Milo, is working with Zayed on his interest in returning to the university to get a degree in law.

Consensus reality level

In the first example, a consensus reality approach to long term edge work is illustrated. Zayed is in his mid-forties and feels he cannot go back to school because it is too late. He has a full-time job, and a wife and children to support. He feels he has neither the time nor the money to go to law school.

A CONSENSUS REALITY APPROACH TO EDGE WORK

ZAYED: Well, it's been a dream of mine to go to law school. When I was younger, I had no money. But now that I have money, I have no time! I mean, it seems silly for a 46-year-old man to go back to the university. Everyone there will be my kids' age!

MILO: I don't think it's that unusual. The number of mature age students has increased dramatically over the years. In fact, I think they even have clubs or support groups for mature age students.

ZAYED: Really? You think I wouldn't be the only one?

The positive feedback – interest, surprise – to the information offered makes Milo think this may be a consensus reality edge. Maybe Zayed needs support, information and encouragement. Maybe the inner obstacle is not necessarily that big.

MILO: Oh yes, I'm sure of it. More and more adults are beginning second careers later in life. I think there's an office at the university that offers help for returning mature age students. Shall I find the number for you?

ZAYED: Yes, that'd be great. Gee, maybe I can even reach them today. It's not yet 5 o'clock.

The relative ease with which Zayed accepts the information is positive feedback. The edge is a consensus reality problem, a lack of concrete information, support and encouragement.

Dreamland level

In the next example, the edge is approached from a dreamland perspective. The signals show that negotiating the edge calls for an interaction with inner figures.

A DREAMLAND APPROACH TO EDGE WORK

ZAYED: Well, it's been a dream of mine to go to law school. When I was younger, I had no money. But now that I have money, I have no time! I mean, it seems silly for a 46-year-old man to go back to the university. Everyone there will be my kids' age!

MILO: I don't think it's that unusual. The number of mature age students has increased dramatically over the years. In fact, I think they even have clubs or support groups for mature age students.

ZAYED: *Looks dejected.* Well, still, I probably won't fit in. Anyway, who wants to hang out with a bunch of old people, anyhow. Even if I got in, I'd feel so isolated because of my age.

Milo thinks the obstacle is "old age," the mind-set of feeling old, depressed and hopeless. The "old people" are in his signals, happening in the moment in the way he gives up so easily.

MILO: *Winks at him.* Yeah, you're a real old timer. Over the hill. No more pep in you, buddy. And all that book reading! That would be too much for your fading eyes.

And I'm not so sure your hemorrhoids and arthritic bones could take all that sitting anyway. Why not just forget about it, take up a hobby and wait for retirement. It's only 15 years away. *This is a forbidding intervention at the edge. Milo paradoxically represents and amplifies the "old people" at his edge.*

ZAYED: *He laughs.* Hey, I'm not that old! OK, OK, I get it. But what if I go there and don't like it. Or I fail?

He's still working on the attitude of old age. Failure feels like an obstacle. A "young" attitude would focus instead on giving it his all.

MILO: What failure? I don't see failure if you enroll and give it your best shot. Even if you don't pass your course, you're a winner because you followed your passions.

ZAYED: You really think I can do it? *He's starting to step over the edge a bit, but the need for support is still part of the edge. He really could fail, but the point of this process is not necessarily to succeed, but to follow a dream.*

MILO: No, I don't think you can do it. *Zayed looks baffled.* And I don't think you can't, either. I'm not thinking in your making it or not. It doesn't matter to me. Are you interested in law school because you think you'll succeed, or because you have a passion for law? Maybe you'll fail, but at least you'll have followed a lifelong dream. That's a form of success in and of itself.

From the perspective of dreamland, money and time are only seen as problems, because of Zayed's edge. The edge creates the appearance of an outer obstacle ("too old"). In this example, "old age" is an attitude that stops Zayed. It is his belief that success is tied to outer accreditation.

Sentient level

At this level of awareness, edge work is "no-edge work." Zayed's signals suggest dreaming and hyperspatial solutions.

A SENTIENT APPROACH TO EDGE WORK

ZAYED: Well, it's been a dream of mine to go to law school. When I was younger, I had no money. But now that I have money, I have no time! I mean, it seems silly for a 46-year-old man to go back to the university. Everyone there will be my kids' age!

MILO: I don't think it's that unusual. The number of mature age students has increased dramatically over the years. In fact, I think they even have clubs or support groups for mature age students.

ZAYED: *He sighs.* It all feels so difficult, though. I mean, three years is a long time. And my family. You know, being a lawyer was always my dream, but I feel so far from that now. *His lack of energy for encountering the edge could be hopelessness, or it might be a signal not to encounter the edge through conflict. He stresses "being a lawyer," the dream pulling him towards his edge. Maybe it is also a method, to dream his way over the edge, not a direct encounter, but tunneling.*

MILO: Ahhh, the lawyer. What's he like? *Milo is looking for the sentient experience of being a lawyer.*

ZAYED: The lawyer? Hmm. *He closes his eyes and thinks for a moment. His posture shifts, and he sits upright.* The lawyer...the lawyer is dynamic. He's going somewhere. He has a... sense of direction.

MILO: Yeah, go ahead, feel that sense of direction. What's that energy like? *Milo is moving away from the figure of lawyer, focusing on the sentient quality of "direction."*

ZAYED: *He pauses for a long time.* Hmm, it feels like a sense of direction, like a focus. Forward. Focused. Doesn't matter where I'm going. Like nothing can stop me.

Zayed's signals are mostly non-verbal. He has difficulty finding words, and describes his experience in terms of energy rather than parts. The sentient approach to this edge is to find the lawyer in Zayed's immediate experience.

These three examples all illustrate methods for deepening an unknown experience or identity. They are methods that can be used in short-term edge work. But an edge is also a long-term process. It often takes more than one session to change directions in life. Often, it takes years to develop a relationship with different parts and tendencies. In the next chapter we will look at long-term edge work, and the structuring pattern of the life myth.

Chapter 8

Life Myth and Long-Term Edges

Life-learning comes through many avenues, both painful and pleasurable. Process Work reflects this understanding in its approach to long-term edge work. Long-term edges are seen as opportunities for learning the central lessons of a person's life, of discovering the life myth, the basic blueprint behind life's meandering path. Our long-term edges may be connected with chronic relationship issues, habitual behavioral patterns, addictions, moods, chronic illness, and other prolonged or recurrent experiences. Some involve facing obstacles and disturbances. Others involve opening up to joy or abundance. While they may take a variety of forms, they always occur as a person ventures further on his or her life journey. In this final chapter, we take a look at how Process Work facilitates long-term change. First we will explore the concept of a long-term edge, and then we will present skills and metaskills that are useful for working with edges over time.

Long-term edges, awareness and life myth

Process Work approaches long-term edge work with a focus on awareness. Resolution of problems is viewed as a by-product of developing awareness, rather than as end in itself. This approach can provide relief from problems, even when they cannot be resolved, by bringing about an expanded viewpoint. Long-term edge work makes the boundaries of identity more fluid and permeable, and encourages the development of detachment, particularly through the practice of seeing the "other" in oneself.

Process Work with long-term edges is influenced by Jung's concept of the life myth. Jung originally coined the term "life myth" to describe a patterning for life-long personal development. He found that childhood dreams, which often stayed in a person's memory into adulthood, revealed an archetypical or mythic pattern for a person's life. Like an astrological chart, the childhood dream was not a predetermined path, but a picture of tendencies, represented symbolically. Mindell extended Jung's work on life myth and childhood dreams by proposing that patterning for a person's life can also be seen in recurrent and long-term experiences, such as chronic symptoms and illness, addictions, and relationship patterns. Mindell sees a life myth as a form of "psychological inheritance," which includes tendencies related to parents, ancestors, cultural context and historical background. A person can work with a life myth consciously and creatively, instead of being propelled by it unconsciously.[42]

Life myth is a useful concept for understanding long-term edge work, because it frames the personal growth journey in an

---

[42] Arnold and Amy Mindell, Quantum Medicine Seminar, Yachats, Oregon, February 27-March 3, 2000.

impersonal way, allowing for wider perspectives and new meaning to emerge. It locates personal history in the context of a broader archetypal drama, and adds a spiritual dimension to self-exploration, by addressing questions such as, "Why am I here?" "What am I meant to learn or do?" or "What is my purpose in life?" Viewing experience as part of a mythic pattern can relieve feelings of stuckness or failure that often accompany chronic problems, and can bring reminders of life's meaning and purpose.

When particular problems and experiences happen over and over again, they provide repeated opportunities for examining core issues. Each time, they bring new experiences, meaning, and insight. As stopping places on the life journey, long-term edges seem more or less the same every time they are encountered. Yet, each time they come around, they bring the potential for personal change and growth. As in mythic tales, the dragon does not change, but the hero does.

An example of long-term edge work and life myth

Working with a long-term edge in connection to a life myth is illustrated in the following example, in which a facilitator, Shawna, is working with a client, Kim, on alcohol addiction. Kim has had a drinking problem for thirty years. She has tried Alcoholics Anonymous, re-habilitation clinics, cognitive-behavioral therapy, and psychoanalysis, but continues to drink. She hates her addiction, and feels it has ruined her life. She has financial difficulties, serious health problems, and has lost touch with some family members. From their work together, Shawna and Kim discover that Kim's drinking is connected to socializing. Her biggest temptation is to stop by the bar on her way home from work. She loves drinking with the guys at the bar. In her sober identity she is very shy and retiring, not given to extraversion. Her drinking brings out another side of her, which she cannot seem to access in a sober state of mind. The challenge of getting sober seems insurmountable to her.

Shawna works with Kim on this addiction for a couple of years. Each phase of their work brings them to a long-term edge. One of these involves addressing the inner criticism, shame, and overwhelming sense of failure that plague Kim. At other times, Kim works on cleaning up her addiction. She also works on bringing more of her outgoing, social self into her everyday life, so this does not have to happen through drinking. In this long-term process, Kim has times when she stops drinking altogether, and even loses her identity as an alcoholic. She also has times when she continues to drink, and accepts herself, addiction and all.

If Kim's progress is measured against a goal of sobriety, all the therapy that did not result in sobriety is a failure. However, if quitting is not the only goal, and the influence of a life myth is taken into account, the therapeutic process looks very different. In the only childhood dream she can remember, Kim is in a big city, and becomes separated from her family. She describes her experience in the dream as "wandering around in this huge crowd of people, strangers. And they were all different, like people from different countries, all different sizes and shapes even. I was fascinated by them." As a result of working on this dream, Kim sees her struggle with alcohol as a journey with meaning and purpose. She realizes how her addiction relates to her family and culture, and how her drinking patterns enable her to bridge cultures and groups. Her socializing is more than just a "hanging out" with others. It is an attempt to connect deeply with a wider range of people.

Working on long-term edges from a mythic perspective connects the purpose of a person's life with the edges that occur along the way. It is often a more sustainable approach to problems. Each long-term edge brings encounters with inner allies, or experiences that are supportive of the life journey. In Kim's case, each failure to stop drinking is a way station on her mythic journey, a new opportunity for learning and growth.

Skills for long-term edge work

Like all edge work, long-term edge work involves helping a client notice experiences that have been marginalized by everyday consciousness. By bringing awareness to these experiences, behavioral changes tend to occur spontaneously, in accordance with the nature and timing of the person's process. Long-term edge work involves noticing the signals of change, as the change is already happening, and thereby gaining a sense of the direction in which to proceed. When someone comes to an impasse, or does not know where to go next, the signals of the dreaming process show the way. The methods that follow are signal-based awareness techniques that can be used in long-term edge work.

Blank access

Use of blank access to negotiate a long-term edge is based on the questions, "How is the edge already being dealt with? What direction is indicated by the signals that are happening right now?" Non-verbal responses provide an organic pattern for the next step. For example, if a facilitator asks a client, "How will this new experience look in your everyday life?" an answer will be found in the client's non-verbal and verbal response. The client might look upwards, visualizing something, make a movement indicating that the experience is already happening kinesthetically, or sigh and look despairing. The facilitator listens for clues about how the process is naturally unfolding, in words and body language, dreams, dreamfigures, stories, memories. Whatever happens in response to a blank access question is a possible direction to follow.

Noticing who shows up at the edge

Long-term edge work is a form of relationship work, since it involves facilitating a client's relationship to upheaval and uncertainty. Some clients become very focused on their process of change, while others give up, or become self-critical when they feel they are not living up to their goals and expectations.

In the following example, a facilitator, "Jerome," works with a client, "Ari," on a long-term edge. The example shows the use of edge work techniques, such as blank access and noticing who shows up at the edge. Ari's presenting problem is a chronic inability to change jobs. Ari hates the job he is in, but is afraid to give it up or look for another one. He regularly thinks about quitting, but whenever he does, he comes to an edge and feels hopeless and depressed. Each time he works with Jerome on the possibility of doing something new, he gets to a point where he sighs, slumps down in his chair, shrugs his shoulders and says, "Yeah, but who knows if it really will be a better job. What if I take this big risk, only to find that the new job has just the same problems as the old one?" Jerome sees that Ari's hopelessness is difficult to do battle with. He finds himself wanting to get him to be positive, have courage, and take risks, but the more he encourages him in that direction, the more hopeless and dejected Ari becomes. Ari's relationship to his edge, and to change in general, is apparently a greater problem than the issue of changing jobs.

Realizing that his own enthusiasm about changing his jobs is in part a dreamed up reaction and is not helpful to Ari, Jerome focuses directly on his client's relationship to the edge. He decides to amplify Ari's signals of hopelessness, to see what is behind them. "Why work on anything at all," Jerome wonders aloud, "if we can't be sure the results are going to be satisfying?" In a sense, this comment is a blank access. Jerome is not sure whether he is formulating exactly the sentiment behind his client's hopelessness, and is hoping Ari's response will show the way.

"Well," Ari says, "it's not that the results have to be satisfying, but it just seems that no matter how hard you try, you can never win. Nice guys finish last," he says with a wry smile. "What do you mean?" Jerome asks. Ari replies, "Well, everyone is out for themselves, and no matter how hard you try, it always seems you get done in by someone else. You just have to go along with the game." Ari's apparent edge to change jobs is connected to a more general edge in life: an inability to go for what he wants. He has long had an identity of being a nice guy, who loses out to others. The "loser" is the one at the edge, the one who stops the process from going forward. And just beneath the surface, the loser is also angry. His fighting spirit, found in the signal of his sarcasm, is probably not something he identifies with. Jerome and Ari must find out more about the identity of the loser and how it became so entrenched, before they can go any further.

Dreaming over the edge

At some point in working with a long-term edge, clients often begin to think about integrating a new identity or experience into their everyday life. They might want to know what changes they might have to make in order to fit a new experience into their everyday lifestyle. Trying to figure this out using everyday consciousness will be only partially successful. A fuller solution comes from including the perspective of the dreaming experience that is trying to make itself known through the problem. For instance, a person who has newly discovered a creative part of her nature may think about new routines, activities, or projects that would allow her to live it out more. But this only involves her everyday awareness. Her creative mind needs to be consulted as well. The facilitator and client might dream together about how life might look once creativity is included, using the creative mind-set that has already emerged from their work together. Directions that emerge tend to be more surprising and more fun than those that focus on programs for change using everyday awareness.

A client from a previous example, "Sushila," wants to live a more artistic life, and suffers from feeling tied to her conventional job and family responsibilities. She works with a facilitator, "Leo," on this long-term edge in various ways. Sushila is able to address various practical matters such as money, organization, and familial obligation. Not feeling entirely satisfied with this, she works on the same edge from the viewpoint of a free, queen-like, dreamfigure that shows her how to live more artistically in her everyday life.

Taking this example further shows how the mind-set of the queen-like figure is helpful for long-term integration. Leo says, "Dear queen, may I ask you a question?" "Certainly, dahhling," Sushila replies, as the queen. "Well," Leo continues, "what shall Sushila do? She wants to be an artist, but has many financial obligations. It looks unlikely that she can just leave her job." The queen looks down her nose at the facilitator. With disdain dripping from her voice, she says, "Sushila thinks it's her job that keeps her from being more like me. Hmmph. Even if she did quit her job, she'd still be a boring, sniveling mouse. She first needs to loosen up, have some fun, and be less predictable and more bizarre. Like me, dahhling."

By this point, Sushila is giggling, even as she plays out the queen. She says, "She's right! I am boring!" and bursts out laughing. "It's not just about painting, though that would be wonderful. It's about everything, it's about how I pour milk on my cereal!" Sushila realizes that the artist she longs to be is an attitude and a lifestyle, not just an alternative profession. Through her work with this long-term edge, she is able to connect her more deeply to the essence of the artist, as a wild, spontaneous, and unpredictable quality that is available to her regardless of what she does for a living.

Doubts, fears and critics

Long-term edge work often requires dealing with reactions to personal change from a client's friends, family and environment. Clients may fear what will happen if they make a change. Their new ways of thinking or behaving may threaten a relationship with a friend, loved one, or co-worker, and they may encounter rejection or criticism.

Certain fears and doubts are a function of the edge itself. Sometimes a facilitator may be tempted to support a client by negating fears, offering reassurance, or predicting positive responses from others. Another temptation is to try to help clients "win" against outside opposition or doubt. Minimizing the possible consequences of crossing a particular edge and taking sides against real or imagined opponents can be useful in working with a long-term edge. It is also important to remember that outer opposition often mirrors the client's own doubts.

A facilitator has no inside knowledge of what will actually happen, when the client tries to live out a particular change. The facilitator cannot be sure that the client's fears will not come true. While she might encourage a person to take a risk, she should also acknowledge the possibility of negative consequences, and help the client address these as well. Edges involve letting go of something, such as the approval of others or the ease of the *status quo*. Helping clients to prepare for this is often a more sustainable way of working on a long-term edge than assuring clients that their changes will be well received.

Outer and inner support

Long-term edge work is a life-long journey. At each stop along the way, a person may need different types of support or resources. Sometimes clients need consensus reality help. They may need to build up their resources by acquiring outer helpers, information, or learning opportunities. Alternatively, difficulty with asking for or accepting help or guidance may prevent people from moving forward. Sometimes they may need to work with inner figures, or aspects of their life myth. By following the signals of the process carefully, a facilitator can assist clients in identifying their needs and how to go about meeting them.

The importance of models as allies

Sometimes making change is difficult because there is no model for the new way of being. A real or imaginary figure can represent something on the other side of an edge. A person, animal, place, or object, a mythical or fantasy figure, or character out of a book, movie or play can serve this purpose. A facilitator can help a client find models such as these by asking, "Who do you know who can already do this?" or "Can you imagine someone who could do this." Another useful question is "What will you be like in twenty years?" followed by the suggestion, "Imagine yourself as that person and see yourself through his or her eyes."

This is illustrated in an example Julie tells, about her experience working as a young therapist in Switzerland. "My client was a young woman in an unhappy marriage who wanted to get a divorce. She had married a few years earlier, at 19, under pressure from her mother, and had never been happy with her husband. She had no support to leave him. I was just starting out as a therapist, and felt really useless. I was very shy, and had trouble talking about marriage and divorce directly. We spent hours talking about her situation, but I never I helped her with her problems. I worried that nothing useful came out of our work together. Years later, I bumped into her while visiting Switzerland. She was happy to see me, and told me that she had eventually gotten a divorce and was living happily on her own, pursuing her career. She thanked me for helping her, and said that our therapy was life changing for her. I was completely puzzled. I asked what she found useful, and she said, 'Oh, well, I loved just sitting and talking with you. You had such an American way about you. You were so spontaneous. It was good for me to be in your company.' I realized that even though I wasn't a very good therapist, I had been able to be a model for my client. Somehow, my way of being in the world attracted her dreaming process, and encouraged her in her own direction."

A hyperspatial approach to long-term edge work

From a sentient perspective, change does not require any edge work. Because sentient awareness is unitary, it is not concerned with parts and polarities, and does not focus on the details of everyday life. In a sentient state of awareness, there are no conflicts, critics, goals, striving, or achieving. There is nothing to integrate. There is only the spaciousness of the immediate present.

One way of working sentiently with long-term edges is to find hyperspatial solutions. A hyperspatial approach to long-term edge work is illustrated in the following example of relationship work, in which a facilitator "Kevin" works with a couple, "Maurice" and "Jack."

Maurice and Jack are seated side by side, but do not look at each other, or talk to each other directly. They face the facilitator instead. When Kevin asks them about this, they both agree that they are scared of fighting with each other. They have had some bitter conflicts in the past and want to avoid hurting each other any more. They say that even though they fight a lot, they feel that deep down they have a strong love for each other.

Following their signals of not facing each other, Kevin decides not to work directly on the conflicts, but to first help them connect to their feelings of love, using sentient methods. He thinks that they may find solutions to their conflicts in a sentient experience.

Kevin asks Maurice and Jack to recall what they love about each other. Using a poetic question to elicit sentient feelings, he asks them to feel the space between them. They meditate on this for a few minutes. After a while, they speak. Maurice says that when he senses what's between them, he becomes aware of a light, relaxed feeling, very easy and untroubled. Jack says that he had a similar feeling. He felt quiet, and peaceful. Kevin then asks them to stay with these feelings, and from there, look back at their conflicts and fighting, and see what they notice.

After several quiet minutes, Maurice and Jack speak about their experiences. Jack says that from that quiet state, he sees that in his ordinary life he is often tense and fearful. He realizes how he takes on too much, without asking for help. Maurice says that he sees something very similar. He notices how caught up he gets in his work and other responsibilities. He loses touch with his feelings. The love between them is a sentient experi-

Exercise 8.1
Long-term edge work

This exercise is designed to help the facilitator tune into long-term edge signals using a blank access technique. It helps focus awareness on the signals that show how to work with the edge, and the learning implicit in working with the edge

1. Facilitator and client sit together. The client describes a long-term edge, framing it as something he or she would like to do, become, achieve, etc.
2. The facilitator asks "How will you get there?" and offers "multiple choice" answers, such as:
   a) Get help
   b) Have patience and just love yourself
   c) Dream about the next step, in fantasy or play
   d) Use discipline and practice
   e) Pray for help
   f) Drop the problem and your identity altogether
   g) Or …. (Ask the client to fill in, and watch the feedback)
3. The facilitator follows the answer the client is most interested in, noticing non-verbal and verbal feedback.
4. The facilitator continues to follow the client's signals. If the facilitator doesn't know where to go next, he or she can ask: "Where are you at now?" or "Where should we go next?" and then follow non-verbal feedback.

The facilitator's goal is to help the client find an inner direction, and appreciate the learning along the way.

ence. By getting in touch with it, they reconnect with the foundation of their relationship.

Metaskills for long-term edge work

Metaskills play an important part in working with long-term edges. An overarching metaskill in working with long-term edges is the understanding that change is a property of nature, and is not something that can be determined by will or desire alone.

Timing and the edge

Edges have their own timing, independent of a client's intention or a facilitator's skill. Respect for the timing of the edge is an important metaskill. Long-term edge work requires an appreciation of the mystery of the moment, and the belief that things change when the timing is right. Facilitators who become over-identified with making change happen cannot differentiate between their own enthusiasm for change in the client, and the client's own desires and motivations. Their interest in change may prevent them from noticing a client's signals of disinterest, fear, or ambivalence about a particular direction. They may push ahead, instead of helping the client to relate to the various parts of a process. This is sometimes harmful to facilitators as well, because it contributes to burnout.

When it appears as though a facilitator is making change, usually this is because the change was imminent in the process. The facilitator may be "dreamt up" to say or do certain things, or take an approach that lets the change loose. Raymond Corsini tells a story that illustrates this in the preface to his book on comparative psychotherapies.[43] A man rushed up to him at a conference, shook his hand vigorously, and with great enthusiasm said, "Doctor, do you remember me? You cured me years ago, and changed my life forever. Do you remember me?" Corsini struggled to remember the man's face, but could not remember him at all. He wondered how he could forget a client whose life he had so dramatically changed. He asked the man when he was his patient. "Oh," replied the man, "No. I wasn't a patient. I was in prison, and you were the prison psychologist. You told me that I had a high IQ score. That

---

[43]Raymond J. Corsini, *Current Psychotherapies*, 4th ed. (Itasca, IL: F.E. Peacock Publishers, 1989), 13.

changed my life! For the first time, I believed in myself. I felt confident, and decided right there, on the spot, to get my GED, get out of prison as fast as I could, go back to school and get a good job." This change was already inherent in the man's process. Corsini's comment was helpful simply because it allowed the client to become aware of something that was already there.

Relating to fate

Instead of pushing for change, a facilitator can help a client relate to a process as an expression of fate, or the Tao. From this viewpoint, integration is about relating to the unknown, instead of trying to tame it.[44] At one of Mindell's earliest classes, where he was first presenting the concept of the edge, someone asked, "Why are there edges?" At the time, the class was held in a conference room of a village hotel. Everyone was sitting along a rectangular table, and Mindell was sitting opposite the person who asked the question. He said, "Well, if you had no edges to reaching out, for instance, you could just reach out across the table and take my hand. But if you had an edge, you'd have to go the slow way, stopping at each individual along the perimeter of the table, until you came to me. It's a slower path, but along the way, look how many more people you would get to meet." From this perspective, an edge is an encounter with fate and a learning opportunity.

Dropping everything

Believing that change happens in its own timing brings surrender, not out of hopelessness, but out of humility. Individual efforts are not always enough. Sometimes it brings the greatest relief to drop whatever has been causing so much struggle or difficulty. The feeling of having to work hard disappears. The

---

[44] Max Schupbach has discussed the idea of relating to one's own process in his classes on facilitation, and in particular, in his class, "Spirituality and Process Work," Portland, Oregon, September–October 2000.

feeling of failure for not getting somewhere melts away. Self-criticism abates, allowing an appreciation of the moment to take over. Sometimes, the attitude that there is nowhere to go, nothing to achieve, and that life is for learning, is the attitude that helps the most.

Sometimes it becomes evident that working hard at change means there is actually no need of change at all, as the following example shows. Julie once worked with a woman who had suffered an abusive childhood. When she came to see Julie, she was 36, and had been in therapy since she was 17. Through that time, she had worked on herself with great effort and intensity. She was now married to a man she loved very much, had a job that she enjoyed, and was expecting her first child. Julie had only seen her a few times. She had come to work on her fears about being a mother, particularly her fear that she would not be able to protect her baby from harm, as she herself had not been protected by her own mother.

One day the woman came late to therapy, which was unusual for her, since each of the previous times, she had been in the waiting room at least ten minutes before her session. She admitted, with embarrassment, that she had forgotten about the session. She got caught up in painting the baby's room and had totally lost track of time. Julie found that an interesting signal, since it seemed unlike her. She asked the client, "What was so much fun about painting that made you forget everything else?" The woman broke out into a huge grin, and began to tell Julie excitedly about the colors she was painting. With great enthusiasm, she described the new furniture and the artwork she wanted to paint onto the walls.

Following her excitement, Julie said, "Gee, I can see why you'd rather stay home and paint. Sounds more fun to me, too!" The client looked at Julie in shock. "What do you mean?" she said. "I *need* therapy. I'm so afraid that I'm not going to be able to be a good enough mother." "But," Julie said, "if you really needed it, wouldn't you have remembered your appointment? Maybe you need it less than you think. Isn't it more fun preparing for the baby, and enjoying this phase of life? Every new mother worries they won't get it right. Maybe you've had enough, for the time being, focusing on your past. Maybe it's time to just look forward to your future?"

The client thought for a moment, and then smiled shyly. "You know," she said. "I've been in therapy for almost 20 years, and I've learned a lot about myself, but I feel bored with it. I mean, I get a lot from it, but I'm tired of thinking about my past." "Right,' Julie said, "why not let go of it for the time being. Why not just enjoy redecorating – you, your baby's room, whatever you want! You can create whatever you want, you don't have to stay stuck in the past!" The woman laughed aloud at the thought of redecorating herself. "Yes, she said, "I think it's time for some fresh new colors, and maybe even some new furniture!" Julie and her client both laughed together, and talked more about the woman's new future, a future that she could design for herself, however she wanted.

Epilogue

In coming to the end of this book, we arrive at a new beginning. We have explored together some of the basic skills of practicing Process Work, and now our paths diverge as we go on to make of that experience whatever we will. Like finishing a bedtime story, it is time to close the book, go to sleep and dream our own dreams! It is time for our own creativity to take over, and show us how to put these skills into practice in our own lives.

Mindell has always emphasized that Process Work is whatever you make it. It belongs to everyone who uses it, and should look different wherever and whenever it is applied. It should carry the "local flavor" of the practitioner and the individual or group with whom she or he is working. By blending your own creativity, personal style, and life myth with the ideas and techniques introduced in this book, you will make Process Work your own, and add depth, color and vitality to the work.

In the introduction we said that this book puts magic in your hands. Now we confess, this is only partly true! Really, the magic is always there, in the dreaming reality that transforms the apparently mundane into something "out of this world." We come to the borders of that dreaming reality countless times a day. The ideas and skills of Process Work that we have introduced in this book simply help us to notice where we already are.

The importance of being aware of the reality of dreaming is illustrated in Carlos Castaneda's account of a lesson from his mentor, the Yaqui shaman Don Juan.[45] Walking with Don Juan in the desert at twilight, Castaneda catches sight of something moving in the bushes. In the dim, shadowy light of dusk, it appears to be some kind of wild animal in the throes of death. Its unnatural and strange movements terrify Castaneda. But as he looks more closely at the creature, he suddenly sees that it is really just a branch moving in the wind. With great relief, he informs Don Juan that it was, after all, only a branch. Don Juan tells Castaneda that he missed a great opportunity, because his dreaming had blown life into that branch. The vision of the wild animal was meant for him.

Process Work's emphasis on valuing the dreaming dimensions of reality makes it more than a way of working on problems. It is also a spiritual direction, a way of living life. Opening up to dreaming experiences allows every experience you have, whether in the supermarket or in the consulting room, to become an access-point for the magical and mysterious parallel world of dreaming. The ideas and skills presented in this book help us to counteract our tendency to discount the dreaming behind the things that catch our attention or disturb us. We hope you will find these ideas and skills useful in furthering your own inner work or professional practice.

Our appreciation of the phenomenal world, and of the dreaming world beyond it, has grown because of this book. We hope this is true for you too. One of the most satisfying things for us, in reaching a conclusion, is that no end is in sight. There is only the next step and the next, arising out of the simple desire to go beyond the bounds of the known.

---

[45] Carlos Castaneda, *Journey to Ixtlan* (New York, Pocket Books, 1974), 101-104.

Bibliography

Arye, Lane. *Unintentional Music: Releasing Your Deepest Creativity.* Charlottesville, VA: Hampton Roads, 2001.

Blofeld, John. Taoism: The Road to Immortality. Boulder, CO: Shambhala, 1978.

De Bono, Edward. *Parallel Thinking: From Socratic to De Bono Thinking.* London: Penguin, 1994.

Castaneda, Carlos. *Journey to Ixtlan.* New York: Pocket Books, 1974.

Corsini, Raymond. *Current Psychotherapies*, 4th ed. Itasca, IL: F.E. Peacock, 1989.

Goodbread, Joseph. *The Dreambody Toolkit: A Practical Introduction to the Philosophy, Goals and Practice of Process-Oriented Psychology.* 2d ed. Portland, OR: Lao Tse Press, 1997.

————. *Radical Intercourse: How Dreams Unite Us in Love, Conflict and Other Inevitable Relationships.* Portland, OR: Lao Tse Press, 1997.

Menken, Dawn. *Speak Out! Talking About Love, Sex and Eternity.* Tempe, AZ: New Falcon Publications, 2001.

Mindell, Amy. *Metaskills: The Spiritual Art of Therapy.* Tempe, AZ: New Falcon Press, 1994. Reprint. Portland, OR: Lao Tse Press, 2003.

―――. *Coma, A Healing Journey: A Guide for Family, Friends and Helpers.* Portland, OR: Lao Tse Press, 1999.

―――. *An Alternative to Therapy: A Few Basic Process Work Principles.* Portland, OR: Zero Publications, 2002.

―――. "A Brief Review of Recent Evolution In Process Theory." *The Journal of Process Oriented Psychology.* Vol. 9, 1, Summer 2004.

―――. and Arnold Mindell. *Riding the Horse Backwards: Process Work in Theory and Practice.* New York: Penguin, 1992. Reprint. Portland, OR: Lao Tse Press, 2002.

Mindell, Arnold. 1984. *Working with the Dreaming Body.* London, England: Penguin-Arkana, 1984. Reprint. Portland, OR: Lao Tse Press, 2002.

―――. *River's Way: The Process Science of the Dreambody.* London: Routledge & Kegan Paul, 1985).

―――. *The Dreambody in Relationships.* New York: Penguin, 1987. Reprint. Portland, OR: Lao Tse Press, 2002

―――. *City Shadows: Psychological Interventions in Psychiatry.* New York: Routledge, 1988.

————.*Coma: The Dreambody Near Death*. Shambhala Publications, 1989 and Penguin-Arkana, 1994. Currently available as an e-book at www.laotse.com.

————. *The Year I: Global Process Work with Planetary Tensions*. New York: Penguin-Arkana, 1989.

————.*Working on Yourself Alone: Inner Dreambody Work*. New York: Penguin, 1991. Reprint. Portland, OR: Lao Tse Press, 2002.

————.*The Leader as Martial Artist: An Introduction to Deep Democracy Techniques and Strategies for Resolving Conflict and Creating Community*. San Francisco: HarperCollins, 1992. Reprint. Portland, OR: Lao Tse Press, 2000.

————. *The Shaman's Body: A New Shamanism for Transforming Health, Relationships, and Community*. San Francisco: HarperCollins, 1993/1996.

————. *Sitting in the Fire: Large Group Transformation through Diversity and Conflict*. Portland, OR: Lao Tse Press, 1995.

————. *Dreambody: The Body's Role in Revealing the Self*. Santa Monica, CA: Sigo Press, 1982. Reprint. Portland, OR: Lao Tse Press, 1998.

————. *Quantum Mind: The Edge Between Physics and Psychology*. Portland, OR: Lao Tse Press, 2000.

————. *Dreaming While Awake: Techniques for 24-hour Lucid Dreaming*. Charlottesville, VA: Hampton Roads, 2000.

————. *The Dreammaker's Apprentice: Using Heightened States of Consciousness to Interpret Dreams*. Charlottesville, VA: Hampton Roads, 2001.

————. *The Deep Democracy of Open Forums*. Charlottesville, VA: Hampton Roads, 2002.

————. *The Quantum Mind and Healing: How to Listen and Respond to Your Body's Symptoms*. Charlottesville, VA: Hampton Roads, 2004.

————. and Amy Mindell. *Riding the Horse Backwards: Process Work in Theory and Practice*. New York: Penguin, 1992. Reprint. Portland, OR: Lao Tse Press, 2000.

Reiss, Gary. *Changing Ourselves, Changing the World*. Tempe, Arizona: New Falcon Press, 2001.

Shapiro, Rhea. "Noticing the Spirits in Everyday Life: Process Work as Spiritual Practice and Antidote to Mild Chronic Depression." *The Journal of Process-oriented Psychology*, Vol.8, 2, Winter 2001.

Waldrop, Mitchell. *Complexity: The Emerging Science at the Edge of Order and Chaos*. New York: Touchstone, 1992.

Paul Watzlawick, Paul, Bavelas, Janet B. and Jackson, Don D. *The Pragmatics of Human Communication: A Study of Interactional Patterns, Pathologies, and Paradoxes*. London: Faber, 1968.

Index

at edge, 128
roles, 94
sentient unfolding, 111-114
synaesthetic, 109, 117
    defined, 115-116
synchronicity, 2, 13, 48, 53, 55,
    56, 108
    at edge, 128, 129

T

Tao, 17-18, 160
Teleology, 3, 6
tense, **49**, 54, 157
tension, 112
thinking skills, **40**
    inductive thinking, **40**
    not knowing, **42**
    noticing bias, **42**
    parallel thinking, 41
    "wicked questions," 43
third attention
    defined, 109
third parties, 48, 54, 56, 57, 58
Tibetan, 116
tone, 54
trance, 51, 127, 136
transcendent
    realities, 12
transformation, 17, 126
troll, 89
tumor, 4
tunneling
    under edges, 145

U

unfinished business, 135
    at edge, 138
unified field, 7
unfolding, **88**, **96**

backward, 109-111
flickering signals, **108**
forward, 109-111
marginalized perception,
    109
sentient, **111**
sentient root, **109**
through role-play, **102**
unknown, **130**

V

verbal, 56
    feedback, 158
verbs, 56
victim, 100, 105
vocabulary, 54
voice, **49**, 54
    as instrument, **69**

W

Worldwork, 9
    seminars, 11
wu-wei, 130

Z

Zeitgeist, 8
Zen, 113

About the Authors

 **Julie Diamond, Ph.D., Dipl.** (Process-oriented Psychology), went to Zurich to study with Arnold Mindell in 1981 and was a founding member of both the Research Society for Process-Oriented Psychology in Zurich, Switzerland, and the Process Work Institute of Portland, Oregon. She was a senior faculty member and former vice president of Academic Affairs at the Process Work Institute, and coauthor of its Master of Arts programs. Julie is the CEO and founder of Diamond Leadership, an international consulting firm that provides leadership and talent development services, including coaching, assessment, and training. Her latest book is *Power: A User's Guide* (2016). She lives in Portland, Oregon.

 **Lee Spark Jones, Ph.D., MAPW, Dipl.** (Process-oriented Psychology), is a licensed psychologist with over 40 years of experience in helping people solve problems, meet learning goals, and achieve positive change. In 2008, following her own path made by walking, she transitioned out of counseling and teaching at the Process Work Institute to pursue her interest in dog psychology and the canine-human bond. Currently she owns and operates a dog training and behavior consulting company in Portland and on the Oregon Central Coast. She specializes in innovative nature-based training and life-enrichment programs for dogs and their families.